POLISH WINGS

Lechosław Musiałkowski

Tupolev Tu-2
Sukhoi UTB-2
Shcherbakov Shche-2

STRATUS

Polish Wings

Wydawnictwo STRATUS s.j.
ul. Żeromskiego 4, 27-600 Sandomierz 1, Poland
e-mail: office@stratusbooks.pl
www.stratusbooks.com.pl
www.mmpbooks.biz
Copyright © 2020 Stratus,
Copyright © 2020 Lechosław Musiałkowski

ISBN 978-83-65958-87-7

Layout concept	Bartłomiej Belcarz
Cover concept	Artur Juszczak
Cover	Marcin Górecki
Translation	Jarosław Dobrzyński
Proofreading	Roger Wallsgrove
DTP	Bartłomiej Belcarz
Colour Drawings	Karolina Hołda

PRINTED IN POLAND

Szczególne podziękowania dla Jacka Borowińskiego za
życzliwość i bezinteresowną pomoc. Dziękuję Jacku.

The author would like to thank Mr Kazimierz Gawron for making records from his personal log book available, with information about the period of his service on Tu-2S aircraft in the 30th Naval Aviation Regiment during 1950–1954, free from propaganda "of the time". I would also like to thank Mr Paweł Gawron for the photographs and information from the period of training on the UTB-2. I also thank Mr Zygmunt Gruszczyk for the photographs and stories from the Sochaczew – based 3rd Long Range Reconnaissance Squadron of the 21st Reconnaissance Aviation Regiment.

The photographs are from archives of Marian Mikołajczuk – including those taken by Zbigniew Chmurzyński, Wacław Hołyś, Zdzisław Szajewski, Janusz Szymański, photographs from the archive of the Air Force Technical Institute, Military Photographic Agency and photographs from archives of Ireneusz Pyrżak and Łukasz Ulatowski via Robert Gretzyngier. The remaining photographs are from the archives of Bartłomiej Belcarz, Jacek Borowiński, Bronisław Firganek, Paweł Gawron, Zygmunt Gruszczyk, Bronisław Grzywnowicz, Wacław Hołyś, Mariusz Konarski, Mieczysław Kowalczuk, Wojtek Matusiak, Andrzej Morgała, Wojciech Sankowski, Tadeusz Starzyński, Wojciech Stasiak, Józef Szwarc, Zbigniew Turosz, Kazimierz Wierzbicki, Konrad Zienkiewicz, author, Polish Aviation Museum in Cracow and Sukhoi Design Bureau.

The author would like to thank Bartłomiej Belcarz, Jacek Borowiński, Robert Gretzyngier, Wacław Hołyś, Wojtek Matusiak and Wojciech Sankowski for their help at various stages of this work.

AVAILABLE

FORTHCOMING

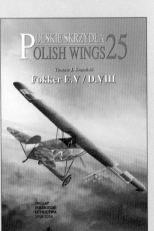

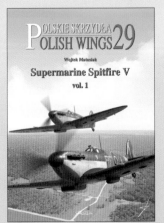

Tupolev Tu-2

The development of the Tu-2 bomber began in the autumn of 1939. The design work on the Tu-2 was preceded by an incident connected with the task to develop a four engine dive bomber given to Andrei Tupolev, by the chief of the NKVD, Lavrenti Beria. Thus in the spring of 1939 Andrei Tupolev was given an unworkable task. According to the idea of the almighty Beria, Tupolev was to develop a high-altitude, four-engine long range dive bomber. Beria's folly was that this aircraft was to be able to attack the British fleet. To be able to attack targets in Great Britain and return to the Soviet Union such an aircraft would have to have a range of 5,000 – 6,000 km. As the flight to the target and back was to be made at the altitude of 10,000 m, the aircraft was to have pressurized cockpits and be powered by supercharged M-105TK-2 engines, designed by V.J. Klimov. This four engine (!) dive bomber with a maximum speed of 635 km/h was to engage targets in a dive with bombs dropped at angles between 50 – 70 degrees at a speed of 900 km/h!

In the opinion of Andrei Tupolev and the engineers of his design team, developing an aircraft in accordance with Beria's imagination was obviously impossible. However, immediate refusal to implement Beria's absurd idea posed the threat of death or deportation to a penal colony. Tupolev's team worked in the Central Design Bureau (TsKB-29) in prison conditions. The TsKB-29 was a special prison within a penal work colony near Moscow, surrounded by a wall with barbed wire. Thus,

being aware of imprisonment on one hand and convinced about the folly of Beria's idea, they however commenced calculation work and construction of a full-size mockup. The project was designated PB (*pikuruyuschiy bombardirovshchik* – dive bomber) or "aircraft 57" (ANT-57). As the high-altitude engines with superchargers were not available yet, the use of available AM-37 engines, rated at 1,400 hp and designed by A. A. Mikulin, was envisaged. In the project PB "57" armour protection of a three-man crew, self-sealing fuel tanks and a neutral gas system were envisaged. For A.N. Tupolev and the team of designers engaged in the PB project, it was obvious that developing a four-engine dive bomber is impossible, as the Soviet aircraft industry was not prepared to build it. Tupolev procured a written report for Beria. He pointed out the great sophistication of this unfeasible project and the ineffectiveness of such an aircraft in combat conditions. Rather than continuing work on the PB project, Tupolev proposed developing a twin-engine dive bomber. Initially Beria reacted with fury for revealing the nonsense of the "wonder bomber" idea and the impossibility to build such an aircraft. With great difficulty, Tupolev managed to convince Beria with his arguments and obtained an order for a new tactical dive bomber, needed by the Red Army air arm.

In the autumn of 1939 the TsKB-29 design team, supervised by Tupolev, commenced work on the new project. It was

[1]: An interesting photograph, both because of the appearance of the Tu-2S, similar to that worn in the period of its service in the 35. PLB and 21. PLZ in 1953 and because of the aircraft displayed along with it. Note the paint scheme and marking details of the bomber, such as red lower tailfin sections and spinner tips, white number "5" stencilled on the tailfin and reversed colour scheme of the checkerboard on the lower wing surface. The Lim-2 "1903" (red tailfin tip is visible), An-2 s/n 16311 and Il-28 "3" (fragments of their wings are visible) and the Mi-1 helicopter are positioned similarly as during the exhibition at Okęcie airfield during 26 August – 9 September 1956.

1

[2]: *Staged photo of a crew in front of a Tu-2S. Standing from right are 1st Lt Eugeniusz Waszyrowski (pilot), 1st Lt G. Cieśla and unidentified gunner/wireless operator. It is visible on the cowlings that the aircraft wears a three-tone camouflage. Inner upper parts of the first two cowling sections and the rear section of the spinner are light grey. The upper part of the last cowling section at the wing is light blue. This colour scheme of the engine nacelle and rear spinner section results from the use of No. 2 variant of the paint scheme, specified in the aircraft's painting instructions. Part of the UPe-2 "S-7" is visible in the background.*

[3]: *A Tu-2S before take-off. Standing in the open cockpit are 1st Lt E. Waszyrowski and 1st Lt G. Cieśla behind him. A canvas cover, used during blind flying training, is visible through the nose glazing. On the top of the antenna mast, with wire antenna of RSB-3bisAD wireless set, the pitot head and outside air thermometer are visible. In the last glazing panel the reflection of a ladder leaning against the cowling, deformed by the glazing shape, is visible. The barrel of a 20 mm ShVAK cannon protruding from the wing root is visible. The forward, vertical support of the underwing bomb rack attached to the fuselage is visible. This photograph was first published in 1954 on a propaganda poster, with cropped lower section to avoid showing the armament.*

project FB (*frontovyi bombardirovshchik* – tactical bomber), also referred to as aircraft "58". The FB aircraft was designed to be a fast bomber, attaining speeds similar to contemporary fighters. Large calibre bombs, carried in the bomb bay, were to be dropped in a dive. The aircraft was to be equipped for day and night operations in all weather conditions. The result of the work was the design of twin engine dive bomber "103" (factory designation "58"). In February 1940 the aircraft's drawings were completed. Simultaneously Tupolev's design team was moved from the prison to Factory No. 156 in Moscow. On 29 February 1940 the Special Technical Bureau (within NKVD), part of which was the Tupolev team, proposed that the aircraft FB 2M-120, also known as "103" be included into prototype procurement plan for 1940. In March 1940 the FB bomber was given the approved designation "103". By the decision of the GKO (*Gosudarstvennyi Komitet Oborony* – State Defence Committee) of 1 June 1940 Factory No. 156 was tasked with construction of three "103" aircraft. These were – as it would turn out later – three different prototypes of a future Tu-2 production bomber.

Construction of the first prototype "103" was commenced in May 1940 at Factory No. 156. It was powered by two 12-cylinder liquid-cooled Mikulin AM-37 inline engines, rated at 1,400 hp with VISh-61T propellers with 3.4 m diameter. The aircraft had a crew of three. The completed "103" aircraft was dismantled and transported to NII VVS (*Nauchno-Isledovatyelnyi Institut* – Air Force Science and Research Institute) airfield at Chkalovsk. There it was assembled on 8 January 1941. After three weeks, on 29 January 1941 the aircraft first flew with M. P. Vasyakin at the controls. Factory trials were conducted during January – May, and in June and July state evaluation was conducted. The bomber, armed with two 20 mm ShVaK cannons and four 7.62 mm ShKAS machine guns, could carry bombs from 100 to 1,000 kg. The maximum bomb load was 2,000 kg. The "103" during the trials attained a speed of 635 km/h at 8,000 m and an altitude of 10,600 m.

The second aircraft, construction of which commenced in July 1940, was designated "103U" after the introduction of numerous modifications, which complied with the requests of VVS RKKA (*Voyenno – Vozdushnych Sil Raboche – Krestyanskeyy Armii* – Air Force of Workers' and Peasants' Red Army). They requested increasing the crew to four. Therefore the forward fuselage section was redesigned to accommodate a widened common cockpit for pilot and navigator, in which the navigator's position aft of the pilot's seat was offset to starboard. In the fuselage a ventral gunner's position was installed. These modifications forced the lengthening of the fuselage by 0.6 m. As in the "103", VISh-61E three-blade propellers with 3.8 m diameter were installed. On 15 May 1941 the "103U" first flew with M. A. Nyukhtikov at the controls. Increased weight caused a slight deterioration of aircraft's performance. State evaluation conducted in June and July 1941 revealed the necessity of improvements in directional stability. This was achieved by increasing the area of the vertical tail surfaces by 1 sq.m. The aircraft was plagued by failures of the defective AM-37 engines. Engine failure was the cause of "103U" crashing on 6 July 1941 at Chkalovsk, after the completion of most trials. The navigator A.M. Akopian was killed. The pilot, Nyukhtikov, bailed out. Engineer Maltsev did not manage to bail out. Despite the crash it was concluded that the "103U" had passed the testing program. On 17 July 1941 NKKP ordered series production of the aircraft at No. 18 Factory in Voronezh. The Voronezh plant was at that time overburdened with Il-2 attack aircraft production. On 19 July A.N. Tupolev and his team were rewarded for developing a successful bomber aircraft with... early release from prison. However, they had to wait for "full rehabilitation" until 1955. In July GKO ordered production of the "103" aircraft in Omsk, Siberia. Factories Nos 150 and 81 were evacuated to Omsk and re-established as Factory No. 166. Tupolev's design team was also relocated there. As early as September the set of technical drawings and documentation necessary for production of the dive bomber, designated "103S", was completed. However, this aircraft did not enter production, but another modification, the third prototype "103V", did instead.

The third prototype was referred to as "103V" (V for *Vysotnyi* – high altitude). It was initially planned to fit it with M-120

engines with TK-2 turbochargers. However, the M-120 engine in inverted Y configuration with three cylinder banks, under development since 1939 by Vladimir Klimov, was still at the stage of uncompleted trials. In fact it failed to pass state trials in August 1941. Therefore it was decided to use in the "103V" M-82 fourteen-cylinder double-row radial engines. Evacuation of the factory to Omsk was delaying and the assembly halls were not completed yet. The prototype "103V" and initial production aircraft were assembled in unheated premises covered with tarpaulins rather than roofs. Tupolev was appointed the chief designer of Factory No. 166 by NKAP. The assembly of the "103V" (aeroplane "60") was completed and it made its maiden flight on 15 December. During joint factory and state trials the aircraft was given the type designation Tu-2 by NKAP on 28 March 1942. Factory and state trials lasted until 22 August 1942. The protracted trials were caused by failures of the unreliable M-82A engines, rated at 1,330 hp. The "103V" could carry a 1,000 kg bomb-load, or a maximum 3,000 kg with reduced fuel load. However, the maximum speed was only 530 km/h at an altitude of 3,200 m. The service ceiling of 9,000 m was also lower than expected.

Series production of the Tu-2 was commenced before the completion of joint state and state trials of the "103V". Its gun armament comprised two 20 mm ShVAK cannons in the wings and five ShKAS machine guns, two of which were fixed, forward firing, mounted on either side of the nose. The bomb load was 1,000 kg, (overload 2,000 kg and with reduced fuel up to 3,000 kg). The first production airframes were assembled from components manufactured in Moscow, originally intended for series production of the aircraft "103U". Initially

[4]: Captain Stanisław Podleśny, a pilot of the 21. PLZ, in front of a Tu-2S at Sochaczew airfield. The spinner tip is red.

[5]: *1st Lt Tadeusz Starzyński (pilot) and 1st Lt Edward Chwastek (navigator) of the 19. Tow Target Squadron(19. LEH) stand on a Tu-2S wing. The same crew during their service in the 35. PLB were based at Świdwin air base as "Świdwin" detachment from 1 February – 31 March 1953, towing target drogues over Mrzeżyno gunnery range during artillery exercises. Landing gear position indicator is visible over the engine nacelle.*

[6]: *1st Lt Tadeusz Starzyński (pilot) and 1st Lt Edward Chwastek (navigator) pose beside a Tu-2S after a sortie.*

the aircraft of the first batch of five examples were designated "103VS". They left No. 166 Factory in February 1942. In April 1942 three production aircraft were sent for evaluation at NII VVS. In September service of a Tu-2 flight began in the 3rd Air Army, which was on the Kalinin Front. The VVS command ordered removal of the nose-mounted fixed 7.62 mm ShKAS machine guns. The ventral flexible-mounted ShKAS machine gun was replaced with a 12.7 mm Berezin machine gun. The second Tu-2 production batch, assembled in April and May, also comprised five aircraft. From the spring of 1942 a UB machine gun was installed in gunner/wireless operator's position. The 3rd, 4th and 5th production batches comprised ten aircraft each. The 6th and 7th batches, comprising 20 aircraft each, assembled from the autumn of 1942, left the factory with the UB machine gun instead of the ShKAS in the navigator's position. Evaluation of three production Tu-2 aircraft, built in the Factory No. 166, lasted until 29 July 1942 at Chkalovsk airfield. The crews consisted of NII VVS personnel. The trials were hampered by failures of the M-82A engines of the "103V" and the first production Tu-2 aircraft. The testing of the "103V" was suspended. To specify the tactical and technical parameters of a production bomber, an example "308"

(100308) was taken from the assembly line. State evaluation of "308" was conducted at Koltsovo airfield in the Urals from 13 September to 28 October 1942, when the aircraft was damaged during an emergency landing. By then it had logged 44 sorties, lasting 32 hours. Following the evaluation it was concluded that the Tu-2 was a modern bomber aircraft, capable of carrying a heavy bomb load. It was stated that the aircraft has long combat radius, potent defensive armament, satisfactory durability and is easy to fly. However, it was noted that the attained maximum speed of 521 km/h at the altitude of 3,200 m was 66 km/h lower than planned. Several other shortcomings, resulting from faulty M-82 engines, were also pointed out. Production of Tu-2 aircraft in Factory No. 166 in Omsk was halted after the completion of the 7th batch. After the completion of 80 Tu-2 bombers it was decided to switch this factory to Yak-7 fighter production.

Despite the halting of Tu-2 production the Tupolev design team continued work on improvement of the bomber's performance and reduction of labour consumption in production. The technologically-simplified aircraft consisted of 72 sub-assemblies. To facilitate transport it could be disassembled into 12 parts. In May 1943 work on replacement of faulty M-82 engines was commenced. The prototype "103V" was fitted with M-82FNV engines (V for boosted) with direct fuel injection. During the trials conducted in July the modified aircraft was 32 km/h faster in flight at sea level (and 23 km/h faster at an altitude of 5,000 m). The test results meant that GKO decided to resume Tu-2 production on 17 July 1943, with improved M-82FNV engines. In two months (July – August 1943) the Tupolev design bureau modified the Tu-2 s/n 716 to the standard being again put into production. It was the pattern for the Tu-2S production aircraft (S for Standard or *Seryinyi*). The Tu-2 s/n 716 first flew on 26 August 1943 and then was quickly sent for factory and state trials. They were conducted during 4 September – 16 December 1943. During these trials the pattern Tu-2S, powered by M-82FN radial engines, rated at 1,670 hp at full military power and 1,850 hp for take-off, with AV-5-167A three-blade propellers of 3.8 m diameter, attained a maximum speed of 547 km/h at 5,400 m. The normal 1,000 kg bomb-load could be increased to 2,000 kg, in the bomb bay and under the inboard sections of the wings. The maximum range was up to 2,100 km and service ceiling was 9,500 m.

In 1943 Tu-2S production was launched at Factory No. 23, previously manufacturing Il-4 bombers. The Tu-2S production was gaining pace, with significant problems persisting during the entire year. The quality of components supplied by sub-contractors was poor, resulting in production delays. In 1943 only 13 aircraft were built. The problems with production delays were solved only in the following year. A total of 378 bombers were built that year, and in 1945 the factory completed a further 742 aircraft. By the end of the war the aircraft industry had delivered 1,216 Tu-2 and Tu-2S bombers. Factory No. 23 produced 43 batches up to the end of the war and terminated Tu-2S production in 1948. In the second half of 1946 Factory No. 166 in Omsk resumed Tu-2S production after three years. Including war production aircraft, the industry delivered 2,527 Tu-2 and Tu-2S bombers.

Tu-2 bombers appeared over Poland for the first time in the spring of 1945. These were Soviet Air Force aircraft, which were redeployed in March 1945 from bases near Moscow to Poznań to take part in the Berlin campaign. Three bomber aviation regiments were then equipped with Tu-2 aircraft: 5. BAP, 815. BAP and 836. BAP. These regiments belonged to the independent 113th Leningrad Bomber Aviation Division (113. OBAD), which was the reserve of the High Command. The crews of the regiments of this division converted from Il-4 to Tu-2 bombers during December 1944 – March 1945. In the spring of 1945 a few Il-4 aircraft were also based at Poznań – Ławica airfield. (Apart from the Tu-2 and Il-4, B-25J Mitchell bombers wearing red stars were also based at Ławica airfield. The 341st Bomber Aviation Regiment of the 4th Bomber Aviation Corps of the Guards was stationed at Ławica airfield from April 1 – May 9, 1945). After the surrender of Nazi Germany the Tu-2 aircraft of the three 113. OBAD regiments were redeployed from Poznań to the Far East, over three days. After eight refuelling stops over the 10,000 km-long route they arrived in Mongolia, from where they flew combat missions against Japan.

The Tu-2 was designed as a dive bomber, but production aircraft were never used in this role. All bombing by the Tu-2 during 1942 – 1943 was performed in level flight. The first production Tu-2s were fitted with dive brakes on the lower wing surfaces. Since the Red Army stopped using the Tu-2 in the dive bomber role, the brakes were removed. Over the course of the production run at Factories No. 23 and 166 the Tu-2S was constantly improved by various modifications. Here are examples of upgrades and other changes introduced during series production:

From the 1st aircraft of the 1st production batch to the 20th aircraft of the 59th batch, built at Factory No. 23 to the 18th aircraft of the 1st batch built at Factory No. 166 the aircraft were fitted with with AV-54-167 three-blade propellers of 3.8 m diameter. Later four-blade feathering AV-9VF-21K propellers were installed. Thus different, larger and more bulbous spinners were also installed.

In aircraft of the 1st and 2nd production batches the fuselage nose section was covered with plywood and from the 3rd batch on only the nose to the 3rd frame was covered with plywood. The rest of the fuselage was covered with 1.5 mm metal skin.

Up to the 44th production batch of Factory No. 23 three circular windows were installed on each side of the fuselage near the ventral gunner's position. Aircraft of later batches had one window of larger diameter on each side. (All aircraft built by Factory No. 166 had single windows).

From the 44th batch on two landing lights instead of one were installed under the starboard wing, and a metal nose replaced the wooden one.

(Plywood nose section of aircraft of the 1st and 2nd production batches and plywood nose and wingtips of aircraft of to 52nd batch was the result of implementation – fortunately at scale reduced by Tupolev – of Stalin's order to spare scarce metals).

From the 45th batch on only single, large windows were installed on fuselage sides, at ventral gunner's position.

From the 50th production batch on the thickness of tailplane skin was increased.

From the 21st aircraft of the 50th production batch from Factory No. 23 and from 2nd production batch from Factory No. 166 the movable section of the gunner/wireless operator's position canopy, called a "turtle", was replaced with a fixed open transparent fairing mounted to the frame and fuselage. The shape of the fairing changed over the course of the production run to a longer one, with flatter upper surface.

Also from the 50th batch on a dished grip on the starboard wing's trailing edge, near the wing root, facilitating climbing onto the wing, was added.

From the 51st batch on a non-slip walkway was added, enabling a safe climb up the wing to the pilot and navigator's cockpit.

Also from the 51st batch built at Factory No. 23 and 3rd batch from Factory No. 166 the main landing gear wheels (1,100 x 425 mm) were replaced with 1,100 x 395 mm wheels with higher tyre pressure and heavier maximum loading. Also from the 51st batch on larger tailwheels (530 x 230 mm) replaced the previously installed 470x210 mm wheels.

From the 21st aircraft of the 52nd batch wooden wingtips were replaced with metal ones.

From the 59th batch on the aircraft were fitted with mechanical de-icers on the wing leading edges.

From the 61st batch from Factory No. 23 on the lower forward nose glazing was asymmetric. On the starboard side there was an additional ventral and side panel. Side and ventral nose glazing reached the forward edge of the bomb bay door. The port side part of the glazing had an opening hatch providing access to the aircraft's systems in this section of the fuselage.

Over the Tu-2S production run the radio communication and navigation systems were upgraded. From the 24th batch the OPB-1R bombsight was replaced with a semi-automatic OPB-1D sight, used in level flight. The OPB-1D sight was coupled with the static and dynamic pressure ports and calculated the aiming angle on the basis of the altitude and speed of the aircraft.

From the 3rd batch on the aircraft were equipped with the SCh-3 IFF system.

From the 51st batch of Factory No. 23 and 4th batch of Factory No. 166 on, apart from the RSB-5 air-to-ground wireless set and SPU-4 intercom, the aircraft were fitted with an additional RSI-6 air-to-air wireless set.

From the 21st aircraft of the 63rd batch Tu-2S aircraft were equipped for instrument flying (ARK-5 ADF, RV-2 radar altimeter and MRP-48 marker beacon receiver). Information about fitting the Tu-2S with an autopilot, often stated in print, is false.

The Tu-2S aircraft were fitted with various types of gun mounts, different in several production batches.

Up to the 47th production batch the navigator's gun position was fitted with BUSh-1 mount with 12.7 mm machine gun, mounted in a yoke on the canopy ring, with 190 rounds of ammunition. The gun position was covered both when firing and during cruise.

From the 48th batch on the VUS-1 mount with the same 12.7 mm machine gun was mounted on a pintle attached to the cockpit floor. On this mount the gun was offset to the aircraft's longitudinal axis. The ammunition supply was 170 rounds. The movable canopy with asymmetric cut-out for

[7]: Two Tu-2S aircraft of the 19. LEH in flight. Visible in the foreground is the tailfin of the UTu-2 with the number "8" painted on the inner surface, which was characteristic of the Tu-2S and UTu-2 aircraft operated by the Long Range Reconnaissance Squadron of the 30th Naval Aviation Regiment. Later, in the Słupsk-based tow squadron, the number "8" was painted on the outer tailfin surface. The Tu-2S "3" of the 19. LEH with winch drum is visible in the background.

[8]: Tu-2S "3" of the 19. LEH in flight, seen from the rear starboard quarter.

[9-10]: A unique series of air-to-air photographs of the Tu-2S "3" taken from the flight engineer compartment of the UTu-2 "8".

Tu-2 aircraft in Poland

Number in air-craft documents	Tactical number
01	1
02	2
03	3
04	4
05	5
06	6
07	7
08 (UTu-2)	8

the gun barrel was opened for firing and slid under the fixed canopy section.

Up to the 44th production batch the wireless operator's position was fitted with VUB-2M gun mount. From the 45th batch on the VUB-68 mount with a different position of the ammunition box was installed. The mounts differed from each other also in the collimator sights (K-8-T or K-20-T) and stabilizers (OMP-6 or OMP-7). Factory No. 166 installed the VEU-1 electrically-driven mount with 250 rounds of ammunition.

Up to 49th batch the ventral gun position was fitted with a LU-Pe-2 mount with 300 rounds of ammunition (Pe-2 aircraft were fitted with an identical ventral gun position).

Tu-2S aircraft produced by Factory No. 23 had 14 fuel tanks with combined capacity of 2,800 l. The aircraft manufactured by Factory No. 166 had two tanks in each wing joined into one, but the total capacity did not change.

After the end of the war with the Japanese, the VVS command stated that the Tu-2 had proven itself well in the frontline (tactical) bomber role. Its designer, A. N. Tupolev, not long ago an inmate in Butyrki prison in Moscow and OKB-29 prison design bureau received the title of Socialist Labour Hero in 1945. However, several years later, when this aircraft was used during the Korean War of 1950–53, it was already obsolete. The Chinese volunteers flying these bomber suffered heavy losses in daylight operations. At this time the speed and defensive armament of the Tu-2 was insufficient in encounters with the aircraft operated by the UN forces.

The military secrecy, which without much sense was extensively applied and strictly obeyed in the Polish armed forces in the post-war years until the 1980s, made obtaining and publishing true information about the number of aircraft in service and their specifications impossible. Therefore in publications of that era information that 15 Tu-2 aircraft were operated by Polish bomber, naval aviation and auxiliary units can be found. Published information that the Tu-2 aircraft "entered the inventory of bomber regiments" was half true, because only a few Tu-2 aircraft were delivered to four regiments, but were transferred from one unit to another.

Also the specifications of the Tu-2 aircraft in these publications were false. Incorrect information that Polish Tu-2s were capable of destroying surface vessels and submarines was published. Due to their Soviet origin, the Tu-2 was assessed as one of the world's best aircraft, without comparing it with similar Western bombers.

Apart from propaganda information, giving the number of Polish Tu-2 aircraft greater than it really was, several unconfirmed revelations also appeared. An example is the statement that the first two or three aircraft in the People's Polish Army, coming from the early production batches, with three-blade propellers, were acquired just after the war as staff aircraft in the Air Force headquarters. A part of this false information,

[11]: *Front view of the cockpit. The pilot, sitting on the port side, did not obscure the view for the navigator, seated behind him. Windscreen wipers are visible on the lower frame of the windscreen. RV-2 radar altimeter antennae are visible on the lower surfaces of both wings. A navigator, 2nd Lt Bronisław Firganek, poses in the pilot's seat. The photo was taken during the aircraft's service in the 19. LEH.*

repeated in several publications, had its origin in erroneous recognition of a fragment of an aircraft with number "01" on the vertical stabilizer in a published photograph. In fact it was a fragment of a Pe-2 aircraft, not a Tu-2!

The Tu-2 aircraft entered service in the Polish Air Force in 1949. On 10 October 1949 eight Tu-2 bombers were handed over to the Polish Air Force representatives at Legnica airfield, operated by a Soviet Air Force unit. These were not new aircraft. They were of post-war production, after a two – or three-year service in the Soviet Air Force. They had undergone overhauls in Soviet repair facilities, necessary after having sustained damage. During the overhauls these aircraft were retrofitted with elements characteristic of late production batches, among others the 61st batch. Two-digit numbers from 01 through 08 were given in the repair facility, without any relation to their previous serial numbers.

Polish Tu-2 aircraft received one-digit tail numbers, "1" through "8", analogous to their two-digit airframe numbers contained in their documents. Published information about Tu-2S aircraft with tail numbers "01" and "9" is not true. No photographs of Polish Tu-2S aircraft with such numbers have been found. There were no such aircraft in the Polish Air Force.

The eight Tu-2S aircraft, with airframe numbers 01 to 08, taken over on 10 October 1949 at Legnica, entered inventory of the 7th Dive Bomber Regiment (7. PBN), based then at Poznań Ławica airfield. The regiment had had this name since 8 December 1948 and then the new name was used in the order of the of the Air Force Commander. The previous, first, name as the 7th Independent Dive Bomber Aviation Regiment (7. SPLBN) had been used since the establishment of the unit in January 1946. The first name of this unit appears in No. 19 order of the

[12 – 13]: Two photographs of the UTu-2 "8" operated by the 19. LEH, taken at Gdańsk-Wrzeszcz airfield in 1958. The crew wear life vests. In the photograph, taken from the rear, the tall mast with antenna of the RSB-3bisAD wireless set and short, angled mast with antenna of the RSI-6 wireless set are visible. On the starboard side the antenna of the SCh-3 IFF is stretched between the fuselage and tailfin. The crew, from left: 1st Lt Zbigniew Turosz (pilot), 2nd Lt Władysław Stępniak and Cpl Zegar.

[14]: A commemorative photograph in front of the UTu-2 "8", taken at Słupsk-Redzikowo air base. The Il-28, tactical number 124, serial number 2115, operated by the 19. LEH during 21 August-17 October 1959, is visible in the background.

[15 – 16]: Two commemorative photographs and also two last ones of the UTu-2 "8", taken in the summer of 1959 at Słupsk – Redzikowo air base. Until the end of the service in the 19. LEH the aircraft had red spinners.

Commander-in-Chief of the Polish Army of 22 January 1946, In an official document of 31 December 1946 another name, "7th Independent Nosediving Bombardment Aviation Regiment", is given, which requires clarification. In "those years" the documents were often created under supervision or in cooperation with people of non-Polish origin. In air units and air force staffs the command positions were usually occupied by Soviet officers, hence contemporary documents are full of expressions borrowed from a language with different grammar rules.

Tail numbers "1" through "8" were painted in white on he vertical stabilizers of the eight Tu-2S aircraft, accepted by the 7. PBN. The aircraft number 08 was referred to in documents as UTu-2. It was fitted with dual flight controls (control column and rudder pedals), installed in the navigator's position in place of the base of OPB-1D bombsight. The trainee occupied the cockpit and the flight instructor occupied the navigator's position. This aircraft with tail number "8", modified in a simple way, was the much-needed combat trainer variant of the Tu-2S. After the acquisition of eight bomber aircraft of a new type, the situation with regiment's equipment did not improve significantly, because the primary type of combat aircraft was still the Pe-2. The Tu-2S aircraft delivered to the regiment were assigned to the headquarters

17

18

[17 – 20]: A series of four air-to-air photographs of the Tu-2S "5" during its service in the 19. LEH. In contrast with "3" and "8", the "5" had an additional blade antenna near the winch operator's compartment. It was operated by the 19. LEH from the autumn of 1955 and was struck off the squadron's inventory in the first half of 1956.

19

20

[21]: *2nd Lt Władysław Stępniak, first from the right, standing to the left of him are the pilot, 1st Lt Zbigniew Turosz and two mechanics from the 19. LEH UTu-2 "8". Świdwin, 1957.*

[22]: *1st Lt Zbigniew Turosz and an unidentified navigator in the cockpit of a Tu-2S from the 19. LEH. Sliding window panel in pilot's compartment is open.*

flight and 3rd Squadron, to which even in October five UTB-2 trainers, transferred from a Soviet unit, were assigned.

In Poland the Tu-2S received the nickname "*Tutka*", quite frivolous for a bomber aircraft. However, if this name was in common use, it was also sporadically used here in the description of this anyway successful and nice-looking aircraft.

The Tu-2S aircraft were for the first time displayed in public during an air parade over Warsaw on 1 May 1950. The parade was led by a Tu-2S, piloted by a Soviet officer, Col. Vladimir Gavrilov, which flew over the stand in Aleje Jerozolimskie avenue, accompanied by two Yak-9P fighters. The leading aircraft was

followed by five Il-10 attack aircraft and five Tu-2S bombers. The parade formation was based at Kroczewo airfield near Zakroczym. There all Tu-2S and Pe-2 bombers were redeployed for the period of preparations for the parade.

The 7. PBN was in possession of seven Tu-2 and one UTu-2 for not very long. In 1950 three aircraft were transferred from this regiment to the naval aviation. First, in February the only UTu-2 ("8") was transferred. Two Tu-2S, "1" and "2", were transferred in late May, because before that the aircraft took part in the 1st May parade over Warsaw.

For summer training from 16 May – 7 June 1950, the entire 7. *PBN* with Tu-2S aircraft was redeployed to Krzesiny airfield near Poznań. Tu-2S crews flew reconnaissance sorties from Krzesiny airfield, also at high altitude (at that time it was 4,000 m). By order of the Air Force Command two crews flew a couple of sorties to take photographs of areas of specified ex-German airfields in the so-called "Regained Land". In the camera bay of the Tu-2S, aft of the bomb bay, an AFA-IM camera for daylight photographs was installed (for night photographs NAFA-19 or NAFA-3S/50 cameras were installed). Bombing was practised at the Biedrusko range near Poznań.

On 11 July 1950 the regiment received a new organizational structure. After reforming two months later it received a new name – 7th Bomber Aviation Regiment *(7. PLB)*. The second public display of Tu-2S aircraft took place on 20 August 1950, during the Aviation Day. A three-ship flight demonstrated an attack on a simulated target on the border of Okęcie airfield. At the end of the summer the regiment was redeployed for training exercises to Leźnica Wielka airfield near Łęczyca. From that airfield the entire regiment bombed targets on the bombing range near Dęblin on 23 September. The first to bomb were the crews of Tu-2S aircraft, which had better radio and

[23]: Airmen of the 19. LEH with seat parachutes. Standing on Tu-2S wing are pilot, 1st Lt Jerzy Konrad (first from right) and navigator, 1st Lt Bronisław Firganek (second from right). Sitting on the fuselage is the navigator, 1st Lt Edward Chwastek.

[24]: Tu-2S "5" with the winch drum visible, during its service in the 19. LEH at Słupsk. The photograph was taken upon arrival at the base of the 30. PL MW (30th Naval Aviation Regiment), after compensation of magnetic deviation and radio deviation of this aircraft, performed there. First from right is a pilot, Ens. Zdzisław Olszewski, holding an artillery compass case. The Tu-2S "5" was briefly operated by the Long Range Reconnaissance Squadron of the 30th Naval Aviation Regiment. It was the most "ubiquitous" of all Polish aircraft of this type. It was operated by six units: 7. PLB, 35. PLB, 21. PLZ, 30.PL MW, 19. LEH and ITWL. Eventually it was donated to the Polish Aviation Museum in Cracow.

[25 – 26]: *Two photographs of an unidentified Tu-2S crew from the 7. PLB.*

[27]: *1st Lt Tadeusz Starzyński (pilot)
and 1st Lt Edward Chwastek (navigator)
in the cockpit of a Tu-2S of the 19. LEH.*

navigational equipment than the Pe-2s. In October 1950 the
7. PLB was redeployed from Ławica to Malbork airfield. The air
component, including five Tu-2S aircraft, flew to Malbork on
24 October. Only the detached component of the 3rd Squadron
of the 7. PLB with Pe-2 aircraft, intended to form the future 21.
Reconnaissance Aviation Regiment, remained at Ławica airfield.

According to the complement, the *7. PLB* should be equipped
with 33 Tu-2 bomber aircraft and three UTu-2 combat trainers
(as well as four Po-2 biplanes). In fact the regiment's strength
was far from the stipulated complement. As of 17 April 1951
the regiment had only five Tu-2S bombers and one UTB-2
trainer. The remaining aircraft in the regiment's inventory were
14 Pe-2s, 2 UPe-2s and 7 Po-2s. This small number of Tu-2S
aircraft never increased, let alone reaching the number specified
in regiment's complement, despite the fact that the deliveries
of new Tu-2 bombers to Poland were to be completed by 1951.
However, re-equipping of the regiment with the Tu-2S aircraft
was halted. (At the same time the Hungarian Air Force received
35 Tu-2S aircraft. They were operated during 1951–1956). In
June 1950 war broke out on the Korean Peninsula and the
hostilities quickly intensified. The parties of the conflict, fore-
seeing its escalation, were preparing militarily for the spread
of the war and the USSR took on an obligation to support
its allies. Therefore Tu-2S aircraft, along with other modern

weaponry, were delivered to the People's Republic of China
and in smaller numbers to the Democratic People's Republic
of Korea. In the latter half of 1950 the USSR sent several dozen
Tu-2S aircraft to its Asian allies. These aircraft with crews, who
had no time to complete a full training course, saw combat in
the Korean War, yet without the expected results. One unsuc-
cessful daylight bomber raid conducted by a larger number of
Tu-2 aircraft is known. Later single aircraft conducted attacks
from low altitude or at night. As result of the Korean conflict,
instead of the expected further deliveries of Tu-2S aircraft from
the USSR… numerous groups of Korean children, war orphans,
were sent to Poland. According to the official version from the
early 1950s, repeated up to now, the halting of re-equipment of
Polish bomber aviation with Tu-2S aircraft to replace war-weary
Pe-2 aircraft resulted from the offer to Poland of jet-powered
bombers by the Soviet Union. Meanwhile the weary Pe-2
bombers diminished dramatically. They were dropping off the
inventory of the only bomber regiment and for two years there
were no replacements. Unreliable, operated without supplies
of new engines and spare parts, Pe-2s eventually gained the
"flying coffin" name. Proof of the bad equipment situation is
Capt. Stanisław Turczyński's refusal to fly the Pe-2. He could
afford it only because he was a Soviet officer. Moreover, the
condition of the 7th Bomber Aviation Regiment was deterio-

rating, not only because of lack of deliveries of new aircraft but also because of the formation of new units at the cost of personnel and inventory. The outbreak of the Korean War and its escalation, bringing the threat of a global war, disrupted the implementation of the seven-year plan of Polish army development for 1949–1955. Instead, implementation of a modified plan of organizational intentions for 1951–1952 began. This plan provided for formation of 15 aviation regiments. On 28 November 1951 the 7. PLB had only five Tu-2S aircraft, one UTB-2 trainer, 11 weary Pe-2s, three UPe-2 combat trainers and two Po-2s in its inventory. This, the only bomber regiment existing, was then reformed. Simultaneously 15th Bomber Aviation Division *(15. DLB)* was formed. From the strength of the 7. *PLB*, personnel to form the 33rd Bomber Aviation Regiment *(33. PLB)* was detached. The new complement for the 33. PLB of 7 April 1951 provided for only two squadrons. The primary equipment of the newly formed 33rd Regiment were old Pe-2 aircraft.

On 22 July 1952 the Tu-2S aircraft took part in the air parade over Warsaw. They took off for the parade flypast from

[28]: *Capts Stanisław Podleśny (pilot) and Teofil Ćwikliński (navigator) in open cockpit of a Tu-2S from the 21. PLZ. After closing the canopy panels the crewmembers still had direct contact with each other.*

[29]: *Cockpit interior with the upper canopy panel hinged to port and two-section side panel hinged to starboard. Sitting in the pilot's seat is a navigator, 2nd Lt Bronisław Firganek. Świdwin air base, 1957.*

[30]: *Capt. Rudolf Gapanowicz with groundcrews of the 19. LEH at Słupsk airfield in front of a Tu-2S. Forward fuselage, cockpit and engine nacelles are covered with tarpaulins.*

[31]: Rear view of a Tu-2S, serving as a backdrop for a commemorative photograph of soldiers, who did not care about the photography ban. Landing gear position indicators are visible on the wings, over the engine nacelles. Świdwin 1957.

the provisional airfield at Kroczewo. Although it was known that the re-equipment of the *7. PLB* with Il-28 jet-powered aircraft was imminent, training of Tu-2S crews was continued on limited scale. In late July five pilots and five navigators of the *7. PLB* were qualified for high altitude operations. In those times flights at the altitude of 4,000 m and above were classified as high altitude operations. However, the training plan was not fulfilled. There was no training to improve flying techniques at night, in clouds and on instruments (in hooded cockpits), due to poor weather conditions.

On 8 August 1952 a fatal crash of the Tu-2S "6" took place. The crew consisted of 1st Lt Kazimierz Staśko (pilot), 2nd Lt Jan Kłosowski (navigator) and SSgt Mieczysław Markiewicz (gunner/wireless operator). The crew was flying a training sortie to bomb targets on the range. On the last leg of the route they flew into a thunderstorm. The aircraft crashed in Jezioro Pakoskie lake. The bombs and ammunition exploded and the crew was killed. The probable cause of the crash was a thunder strike, when the aircraft was descending through the cloud cover.

During 1 May – 1 December 1952 the 35th Bomber Aviation Regiment was formed in compliance with the new complement. Its structure was similar to the *33. PLB*. Apart from Pe-2 aircraft the new *35. PLB* was equipped with three Tu-2S aircraft (tail numbers "3", "4" and "5"). They were transferred in the autumn of 1952 from the *7. PLB*. The only Tu-2S, tail number "7", remaining in the inventory of the *7. PLB* was rarely flown due to lack of spare parts and was eventually scrapped in late 1953. Initially it was expected that the *35. PLB* would receive Tu-2S aircraft in numbers compliant with establishment No. 6/131. Deliveries of Tu-2S aircraft to Poland were to be completed by 1951. Late 1952 was the beginning of the jet age in Polish bomber aviation – re-equipping with Il-28 aircraft. Re-equipping of two regiments – *7. PLB* and *33. PLB* – was

planned. It was expected that the *35. PLB* would continue operating three Tu-2S aircraft and old, weary Pe-2 aircraft until re-equipment with new Il-28 aircraft in 1954.

For two weeks, from 15 to 30 June 1953, a Tu-2S crew from 35. PLB, 2nd Lt Zygmunt Michnowski (pilot), 1st Lt Bernard Gabis and 2nd Lt Władysław Sucharzewski (gunner/wireless operator), was delegated to take part in the tactical exercises of the 5th Air Defence Fighter Aviation Division. The division was based at Warsaw Babice airfield. The delegated Tu-2S crew simulated enemy aircraft for the trainee fighter pilots. In early February 1953 two crews of Tu-2S aircraft (tail numbers "3" and "5") from the *35. PLB* were assigned to support anti-aircraft artillery at Mrzeżyno range. The crews redeployed from Inowrocław to Świdwin airfield. They were stationed there until the end of March as the "Świdwin" detachment. 1st Lt Zdzisław Szczucki was appointed the detachment commander. The crew of the first aircraft comprised 1st Lt Zdzisław Szczucki (pilot), 1st Lt Marian Szulc (navigator) and W/O Stefan Ziomek (gunner/wireless operator). The other crew comprised 2nd Lt Tadeusz Starzyński (pilot), W/O Edward Chwastek (navigator) and Cpl Barczak (gunner/wireless operator). The aircraft towed target drogues, at which the practising AAA units fired over the range. During May-August 1953 three Tu-2S crews from the *35. PLB* were detached as a target tug flight. Two crews supported the gunnery exercises at Mrzeżyno range. The first crew comprised Capt. Eugeniusz Wielkoszewski (pilot), 1st Lt Marian Szulc (navigator) and W/O Stefan Ziomek. The other crew comprised 1st Lt Leon Jędrzejczyk (pilot), 1st Lt Kokot (navigator) and SSgt Jaworowski. The third Tu-2S crew, comprising 2nd Lt Starzyński (pilot), 2nd Lt Szczerba (navigator) and SSgt Biszof, was tasked with target towing at Ustka gunnery range. The Tu-2S aircraft were redeployed to Wicko Morskie airfield. The aircraft were adapted for this task. The redundant

[32]: *UTu-2 "8" of the 19. LEH. The aircraft has no winch drum beneath the fuselage. A flight engineer, 2nd Lt Władysław Stępniak, poses, leaning on the elevator. Świdwin air base, 1957.*

VUS-1 gun mounts with 12.7 mm machine guns were removed and target winches with steel towing lines were installed. The wireless operator/gunner was the winch operator, controlling the drum's rotation speed. The drogue, towed on a several hundred meter long cable, flew much lower than the tug aircraft. After the completion of the gunnery exercise over the range and unreeling the line from the drum, the rotation speed of which was controlled by a hydraulic brake, the navigator gave the command to drop the drogue. The line with drogue was dropped from an altitude of about 50 m.

During the air parade over Katowice on the occasion of the feast of 22 July 1953, a flypast of Il-28 jet bombers from the 7. PLB and 33. PLB was demonstrated (the author deliberately did not use the communist name of that city – Stalinogród, imposed for three years during the peak of Stalinism). The parade was opened by the Tu-2S "5" from the 35. PLB, piloted by the regiment commander, Maj. Kazimierz Wierzbicki, fly-

[33]: *UTu-2 "8" of the 19. LEH at Świdwin air base. The new shape of the digit "8" is visible. Propeller blades and antenna mast of the Tu-2 "3", obscured by tarpaulin-covered Lim-2 and Lim-5 aircraft, are visible in front of the aircraft's nose in the background.*

ing as the leading aircraft. The spare aircraft was the Tu-2S "4" with the crew of 1st Lt Zdzisław Szczucki. Both aircraft, with the entire bomber component, were redeployed to nearby Mierzęcice airfield for the duration of the parade.

In the autumn of 1953 three Tu-2S aircraft were transferred from the *35. PLB* to the 21st Reconnaissance Aviation Regiment *(21. PLZ)*, based then at Poznań Ławica airfield. Along with the sole UTB-2, s/n 3811810, they were assigned to the 3rd Long Range Reconnaissance Squadron of that regiment. At that time the squadron was commanded by Capt. Tadeusz Antonicki. In May 1954 the *21. PLZ* along with the Tu-2S aircraft of the 3rd Squadron, tail numbers "3", "4" and "5", and one UTB-2 was redeployed to Bielice airfield near Sochaczew. Tu-2S, UTB-2 and Pe-2 aircraft of the 3rd and 4th Long Range Reconnaissance Squadrons were ferried to Bielice airfield. Also the jet-powered Yak-23 fighters of the 2nd Close Reconnaissance Squadron landed for the first time at that airfield. The 3rd Long Range Reconnaissance Squadron of the *21. PLZ* operated the Tu-2S aircraft for a brief time, until 1954. Despite this the pilots and navigators, assigned to the regiment after having graduated from No. 5 Officer Flying Training School at Radom and flying the Tu-2S aircraft received the 3rd class of skill level. Among them were a pilot, 2nd Lt Jan Pietraszko and navigator, 1st Lt Teofil Ćwikliński. The maintenance personnel and the first group of pilots from the *21. PLZ* were trained on jet aircraft at Modlin in October 1954. On 18 December 1954 the regiment was renamed 21. *Pułk Lotnictwa Rozpoznawczego (21. PLR)*. In May 1955 the regiment accepted the first four

Il-28R aircraft. They landed at Sochaczew air base on 20 May. Therefore the Tu-2S were soon struck off the inventory of the Long Reconnaissance Squadron of the *21. PLR*. The Tu-2S "4" was decommissioned and scrapped at Dęblin. Also in 1954 the Pe-2 aircraft were retired from the *21. PLR* and the unit's only UTB-2 was transferred to the Officer Flying Training School at Dęblin.

Another unit operating the Tu-2S aircraft was 19th Tow Target Squadron(19. *Lotnicza Eskadra Holownicza – 19. LEH*). It was organized by order of the Chief of the General Staff No. 0138/Org on the basis of the previous tow target flight based at Świdwin. It was established by the order of the Minister of Defence No. 095/Org of 23 August 1954. Two crews of the *35. PLB*, which had been previously staying at Świdwin on a training deployment, flying two Tu-2S aircraft adapted for the target tug role, were assigned to the flight. (As early as 1953 a tow flight from *35. PLB* with two Pe-2 aircraft was based at Wicko Morskie airfield. The Pe-2 "15" was flown by 2nd Lt Tadeusz Starzyński, who later flew in the *19. LEH*. The *19. LEH* operated a total of three Pe-2 aircraft and the Pe-2 "8" was in squadron's inventory from October 1954 until 1956). The aircraft of the newly-formed tow squadron were based at Świdwin airfield from 21 October 1954. In the autumn of 1955 the Tu-2S "5" and UTu-2 "8" were transferred from the Long Range Reconnaissance Squadron of the 30th Naval Aviation Regiment *(30. PL MW)* to the *19. LEH*. The aircraft "3" and "5" were soon retrofitted with improved winches for target drogue towing. The drum of the winch was mounted beneath

[34]: *Close-up of the Tu-2S "5". New paint and checkerboard, properly painted on the starboard wing, are visible. Spinner tips are red. On the left a LWD Żuraw airplane is visible in the background.*

the fuselage, in place of the removed ventral gun station. The gunner/wireless operator's compartment was now occupied by the winch operator. In Polish Tu-2S aircraft the ventral gun was never used – there was no such position in the Tu-2S crew complement. Therefore at the beginning of the Tu-2S service in Poland the 12.7 mm machine guns were removed from this station on all aircraft. Crews of Polish Tu-2S aircraft comprised three airmen, like the Pe-2 crews.

In the spring of 1956 there was an accident of a Tu-2S (number unknown) with pilot 1st Lt Stanisław Widawski and navigator, 1st Lt Leopold Maciejewski, which made a forced belly landing at Sławoborze, 15 km from Świdwin. The aircraft completely ran out of fuel because the pilot failed to monitor the fuel gauges. The crew suffered no injuries. The aircraft required only minor repairs and was brought back into service. (Zbigniew Turosz account).

[35]: Part of Tu-2S "5" is visible in the background of the commemorative photo of a cadet officer, posing in front of the Il-28 "3". s/n 2107. Display at Warsaw Okęcie airfield, 1956.

[36]: Photograph of the Tu-2S (ex "5"), published several times and described as taken during th display at Okęcie airfield in 1956. Note the lack of the number "5" and red lower tailfin section, as well as correct colour sequence of the port wing checkerboard.

In 1956 the Tu-2S "5" was struck off the squadron's inventory. It was transferred to the Military Aviation Works No. 2 *(WZL-2)* in Bydgoszcz, where it underwent overhaul combined with conversion of the winch operator's position to a test bed for ejection seats, used in jet aircraft. The converted aircraft was test flown by a crew of the *19. LEH* – 1st Lt Zbigniew Turosz (pilot) and 2nd Lt Bronisław Firganek (navigator). According to his account, 1st Lt Zbigniew Turosz flew his last three flights on the Tu-2S ex "5" in August 1956. The aircraft opened the air show at Okęcie airfield, held probably on the occasion of the Aviation Day. On the two training flights the navigator was Col. Rozumski from the Bomber Division HQ. During the third, display, flight 1st Lt Chwastek was the navigator and Col. Rozumski supervised the flypast from the ground command post. After the display flight the Tu-2S "5" landed at Kroczewo airfield, where it was taken over by the personnel of the Air Force Technical Institute. After the flight display this Tu-2S was exhibited in the static display.

In 1957 the *19. LEH* received two Il-28 aircraft, tail numbers "122" and "19", fitted with R-1500 winches installed in the bomb bay. Apart from the Il-28 jet aircraft, Tu-2S "3" and UTu-2 "8" were still operated. The UTu-2 "8" was not fitted with a winch. It was used for so-called "silhouette flights" during the anti-aircraft artillery exercises at Wicko Morskie gun range. The gunners did not fire their guns, but practised aiming at the aircraft flying by.

[37-38]: The Tu-2S ex "5", modified for ejection seat tests, displayed at Cracow aircraft exhibition in 1964. The spinners were repainted red and white. The number "5" is lacking. A dent on the port engine cowling, sustained during transport over the bridge in Białobrzegi, is visible. The Yak-11 "36" is visible in the background.

On 28 October 1958 the *19. LEH* was moved from Świdwin to Słupsk-Redzikowo air base, located near Ustka (Wicko Morskie) gunnery and bombing range. Over this range target towing sorties for AAA and the Navy were usually flown.

In 19th Squadron's new combat line-up, established on 23 February 1959 in the 1st Bomber Flight, apart from the crew of the commander, Capt. Wojciech Stasiak, whose assigned aircraft was the Il-28 "22", there were also two crews flying the Tu-2S "3" and UTu-2 "8".

In March 1959 Tu-2 crews flew sorties over Wicko Morskie gunnery range, lasting 9 hours 25 minutes in total. Apart from these, Tu-2 aircraft flew 11 sorties over Mrzeżyno gunnery range, lasting in total 19 hours 19 minutes.

In April 1959 a Tu-2 crew flew only one target towing sortie over the Wicko Morskie range, for an artillery unit training there. In May nine Tu-2S target towing sorties over Wicko Morskie range and one over Koszalin for the local artillery unit were flown. In July flight time on one of two squadron's Tu-2S expired and the aircraft was awaiting an engine change. Only two aircraft remained for target towing over the range: one Tu-2S with 70 hours remaining flying time and one Il-28 with 73 hours remaining flying time.

After organizational changes in the *19.LEH* in October 1959 the 1st Technical Flight had three Il-28 aircraft, one UIł-28 and two Tu-2S, numbers "3" and "8". In the aircraft inventory of 21 December 1959 the same Tu-2S numbers "3" and "8" are listed. According to pilot Tadeusz Starzyński's log book, the last operational sorties of Tu-2S in the *19. LEH* were flown in 1959. During this year Starzyński logged 75 sorties, lasting in total 117 hours and 41 minutes. In 1960 the Tu-2 aircraft were no longer used. On 2 January 1960 the Tu-2S "3" and UTu-2 "8" were withdrawn from the inventory of the *19. LEH*. The squadron was equipped with two Il-12 aircraft, tail numbers "001" and "002", adapted for target drogue towing.

The UTu-2 "8" was flown by the *19. LEH* as late as 1961. In 1961 Capt. Tadeusz Starzyński logged three sorties, lasting in total 1 hour and 41 minutes, in this aircraft. These were two short test flights and a ferry flight to Warsaw. The test flights were necessary, because the aircraft number "8" had been already withdrawn from use and had the control surfaces partially dismantled. The aircraft was brought back to airworthy status. The last, historic flight of the UTu-2 "8" was made in 1961 by a crew of the *19. LEH*, 1st Lt Tadeusz Starzyński (pilot) and 1st Lt Bronisław Firganek. This crew ferried the last aircraft of this type from Słupsk-Redzikowo to Warsaw-Bemowo airfield (entry in Capt. Starzynski's log book).

In 1961 the UTu-2S "8" was officially transferred to the Air Force Technical Institute (*Instytut Techniczny Wojsk Lotniczych – ITWL*). After an overhaul conducted by Military Aviation Works No. 2 *(WZL-2)* in Bydgoszcz, it was used for five years for heavy bomb qualification testing. The tested bombs were dropped at Ślubowo bombing range. After several years of operation by the *ITWL* there were sometimes short circuits in the electric system of "8", which caused accidental opening of the suspension hooks in the bomb bay. Luckily the bomb was not dropped on the road from Przasnysz via Krzynowłoga Mała to Janów, next to which the Ślubowo bombing range was located. Therefore, after this event further use of the UTu-2S

"8" was abandoned and the aircraft was donated to the Polish Army Museum in Warsaw.

The date and location of the first public display of the Tu-2S is depicted in the photos on page 43. They show the Tu-2S "5" in an aircraft exhibition. It is displayed with two 12.7 mm machine guns in the navigator's and gunner/wireless operator's positions. The checkerboards on the lower wing surfaces have inverted colour scheme. The white number "5" below the correctly painted checkerboard was stencilled without painting over blank spaces. Lower, outer parts of the tail surfaces and spinner tips are red, as during earlier service of this aircraft in the 7. PLB and 35. PLB. In the background, to the right of the Tu-2S, "5" the *Żuraw* (Crane) aircraft SP-GLB is standing. In the immediate vicinity of the Tu-2S, An-2 and Il-28 aircraft are standing (as during the air show in 1956).

On the aircraft exhibition held on the occasion of the Aviation Day, celebrated on 26 August 1956, there was a converted Tu-2S as test bed for ejection seats, installed in place of the winch operator's compartment. After the conversion the aircraft had no tail number on the tailfins, though itt still had red spinners. The checkerboards on the lower wing surfaces were painted correctly. The Tu-2S "ex 5" was standing near the Il-28 bomber, tail number "3", serial number 2107, shown in public for the first time, next to the An-2, serial number 16311, with propeller with wooden, "sabre" blades. The open air aircraft exhibition, near Polish Airlines LOT passenger terminal at Okęcie airport, lasted from 26 August till 9 September 1956.

The Tu-2S tail number "5", withdrawn from service in the *19. LEH*, was transferred in 1956 to the Air Force Technical Institute. It was first overhauled at the Military Aviation Works No. 2 *(WZL-2)* in Bydgoszcz, where the winch operator's compartment was completely rebuilt. The canopy was removed, only a small, metal windscreen was retained. The wireless set was also removed. In the open cabin an ejection seat from a Yak-23 (in other publications information that it was an ejection seat from a MiG-15 can be found). After the last overhaul the aircraft was not marked with its previous tail number "5". The operation of the seat, ejected from the Tu-2S flying at an altitude of 1,000 m, was demonstrated by test parachute jumper Capt. Tadeusz Dulla. After the ejection the jumper separated from the seat and descended by parachute. At least one sortie with ejection over water was flown over the Bay of Puck. During the first three flights with Capt. Dulla, the Tu-2S "ex 5" was piloted by 1st Lt Turosz of the *19. LEH*. Navigators on these sorties were alternately 1st Lt Chwastek and 1st Lt Firganek, both still serving in the *19. LEH*. During the first sortie the ejection did not succeed because the firing pin failed to strike the cartridge ejecting the seat, which remained on the test bed with the jumper. Capt. Dulla experienced moments of horror, because the ejection seat could have fired anytime during the flight or, even worse, on landing, actuated by shocks from the landing gear. Later, during service in the ITWL the Tu-2S "ex 5" was flown by a pilot named Smuga.

Two Tu-2 aircraft are preserved in museums in Poland. In the Polish Aviation Museum in Cracow, the repainted ex "5" is displayed. The Tu-2S "5" was delivered to Poland after two years of service in the Soviet Air Force. It flew with the 7. *PLB*, 35. *PLB*, 21. *PLZ*, 30. *PL MW* and 19. *LEH*. In the Polish Army

Museum in Warsaw the UTu-2 "8" is displayed in the open air exhibition.

In 1950 the Naval Aviation started operating Tu-2 aircraft. First, in February the UTu-2 "8" was transferred from Poznań-based 7. *PBN*. In late May two Tu-2S aircraft, tail numbers "1" and "2", arrived from the 7. *PBN* and were assigned to the newly-formed Long Range Reconnaissance Squadron, which became a part of the 30. Naval Aviation Regiment *(30. PL MW)*. Despite the efforts of the Polish Navy command, the UTB-2 aircraft was not transferred from the 7. *PBN* to the Long Range Reconnaissance Squadron. After having handed over the regiment's only UTu-2 trainer to the *30. PL MW* it was decided in the 7. PBN to retain the UTB-2, s/n 3811810, for training purposes. The naval crew, sent to Poznań to collect the aircraft, returned to Słupsk without it. The UTB-2 was eventually not transferred to the Naval Aviation. The crew had to return to Słupsk by train, as the disappointed navigator Kazimierz Gawron recollected.

The Naval Aviation eventually received only three Tu-2 aircraft. The plans were more ambitious. Forming of the Naval Aviation Long Range Reconnaissance Group *(Morski Dywizjon Lotniczy Dalekiego Rozpoznania)* was planned in 1949. It was assumed that the staff flight and long range reconnaissance squadron of this group, equipped with ten Tu-2S and one UTu-2, will be based at Wicko Morskie. The Tu-2S squadron was intended to fly long range reconnaissance missions over Danish and Swedish ports and the entire Baltic Sea. The other squadron, equipped with four heavy and six light seaplanes,

was to be based at Puck. The possibility of delivery of such aircraft from the USSR was taken into consideration and the requirements for these aircraft were specified. It was assumed that "license-built GST flying boats or Consolidated PBY-5A and PBY-6A amphibious aircraft from the Lend-Lease deliveries could be considered". Another plan, known as "Initial plan of rearmament of the Armed Forces for 1948 – 1954" called for equipping the Naval Aviation with 60 maritime aircraft, including 40 torpedo aircraft! However, it was not specified whether it was about Tu-2T aircraft, capable of carrying one or two torpedoes (in 1950 the Soviet Navy still had three torpedo and mine-laying aviation regiments, operating Tu-2T torpedo bombers. Some were purchased by the Bulgarian Air Force, where they equipped one regiment – 25. MTAP, i.e. 25. *Mino – Torpednyi Aviatsyonnyi Polk* – 25. Minelaying and Torpedo Bomber Aviation Regiment).

As it turned out, the plans for the purchase of such a large number of maritime aircraft were void. Before the collapse of the Soviet Union, probably nobody in Poland knew that production of GST aircraft at Taganrog was terminated as early as 1940 after having built only 27. Production of these successful aircraft (license-built versions of the Consolidated PBY-1 Catalina) was too sophisticated and labour-intensive for the capabilities of the Soviet aircraft industry at that time. The few GST flying boats that survived the war were adapted for operation by *Aeroflot* and *Glavsevmorput* in the north of the USSR. Under the Lend-Lease Act only a few PBY-5A amphibious aircraft were delivered to the USSR. The PBY-6A long range,

[39]: *A photograph of the Tu-2S ex "5" taken at the Cracow aircraft exhibition, in which other exhibited aircraft are also visible: Yak-12M "09", Yak-17V "02", Lim-1 "108", Lim-2 "410", Il-28 "25", Yak-23 "16" and TS-8 Bies "0428". The Tu-2S obscures the Yak-11 "36".*

39

radar – equipped amphibians, with 20-hour endurance, remaining in post-war service were too valuable for the Soviets to get rid of them. They were being gradually replaced with Beriev Be-6 flying boats. The PBY-6A amphibians were withdrawn from naval aviation units in the Baltic Sea between September 1953 and May 1954. They were operated in the Black Sea until October 1955 and in the Pacific Fleet as late as August 1957. Perhaps little known is the fact that 14 very useful PBY-1 Nomad seaplanes (the final, improved version of the PBY-6) were fitted with Ash-82FN engines with cowlings and spinners from Tu-2S bombers, to extend their service in the polar aviation. Instead of AV-9VF-21K propellers with square blade tips, typical for the last Tu-2S production batches, four-blade AV-9-21K propellers were installed. The conversion was done at Krasnoyarsk in 1949. The aircraft after these modifications were designated KM-2 and operated until 1957.

The Tu-2S aircraft assigned to the Naval Aviation in Poland were for the most part operated as reconnaissance and bomber aircraft, in contrast with those which were briefly operated by other combat or auxiliary units. In contrast with nine Pe-2 bombers, operated by the 30th Naval Aviation Regiment, in the 1950s the Tu-2S were definitely safer and, in a way, more modern aircraft. Three Tu-2S transferred to the Naval Aviation were in relatively good condition. Flying them was perceived as a great honour. Training on the Tu-2S bombers commenced in the first part of May 1950. The first flights on this aircraft were made by the regiment's CO, Cdr Stanisław Turczyński (a Soviet officer). Crews undergoing training first flew a couple of sorties on the only UTu-2, tail number "8". As in the Air Force, the Tu-2S crews in the 30th Naval Aviation Regiment comprised three airmen, without the ventral gunner. The UTu-2 "8" was assigned to the staff flight, while the remaining two Tu-2S aircraft, tail numbers "1" and "2", were assigned to the 1st Flight of the Long Range Reconnaissance Squadron.

The first air base where the *"Tutkas"* commenced their service in the Naval Aviation was Redzikowo, near Słupsk. At that time it had no paved airstrips and taxiways. A concrete apron on the edge of the airfield was the parking area for Pe-2 and Tu-2 aircraft. During flying days the ground crews were doing there preflight inspections of aircraft scheduled to fly that day, running up engines at take-off power, checking the magnetos and generators. The grass airfield was soggy during the spring thaw and autumn rains. Therefore there were problems with pulling the aircraft out of the muddy ground, particularly the Tu-2S, which were heavier than the Pe-2s. The unpaved surface of the airstrip made the take-off run longer. Moreover, the forest rising beyond the end of the runway compromised safety of the take-offs. The commander of the Long Range Reconnaissance Squadron, Navy Lt Petr Usov, experienced it when his Pe-2 returned to base with pieces of a pine tree stuck in the landing gear after take-off in such conditions. After this incident the airstrip was not paved, but the pines rising on the runway extension were cut down. During the period of stationing of the Tu-2S aircraft at Słupsk the land bombing range of Smołdzino near Lake Gardno was used for single aircraft bombing exercises. The initial point of the bombing run to that range was over the village of Smołdzino (currently the territory of Słowiński National Park.

On 11 August 1950 a Tu-2S, piloted by LTJG Edward Mataczun took off on a practice level bombing sortie at Smołdzino range. Just after completing the traffic pattern over the base and heading for the bombing range, the gunner reported to the pilot that "something is leaking from the port wing". Just after that the navigator, Ens. Kazimierz Gawron, also saw a streak of fluid, dripping from the wing trailing edge just at the engine cowling, sprayed by the air stream. Gasoline was leaking near the hot exhaust stacks of the port engine, threatening the possibility of fire or explosion. In the bomb bay was a load of practice bombs, intended to be dropped on the range in three or four bombing runs. The bombing range was close and the pilot decided to get there, drop the bombs and return to Redzikowo airfield. The jettisoned bombs fell beyond the border of the range. The air swirl after opening the bomb bay door caused fuel spray to penetrate into the cockpit. Opening the navigator's machine gun position canopy helped a little. The pilot decided not to switch off the port engine but to return to the airfield on both engines and he luckily succeeded. The dangerous situation, which could have ended in a fatal crash, was the rupture of the port wing fuel tank. It was caused by incorrect operation and maintenance of the aircraft, not by any technical defect of the tank. In the Tu-2S the fuel tank was suspended on steel tapes, attaching it to the longerons. During maintenance the tank was removed and installed again incorrectly, therefore the steel tapes held it in the wrong places. The fuel was leaking to the space between the tank walls and the rubber sealant. The sealant had been tight for some time, but shocks during take-offs and landings caused it to start leaking. The fuel was leaking to the wing and then outside.

In May 1951 the 30th Naval Aviation Regiment was permanently deployed to Babie Doły air base, vacated by the 3rd Fighter Aviation Regiment. On 3 May 1951 the air component of the Long Range Reconnaissance Squadron with Tu-2S aircraft departed Słupsk-Redzikowo airfield. Interestingly the squadron's documents were placed by the squadron's chief of staff in the engine nacelles of the Tu-2S flown by the squadron commander. At Babie Doły air base he got them out like letters from a mailbox. After the deployment to Babie Doły, the regiment's bombing range was the Bay of Puck, with a permanent target in the form of the stranded wreck of Polish warship ORP Gryf, sunk in September 1939. The wreck was clearly visible from the air and served as a bombing and gunnery target. In the Bay of Gdańsk area the Tu-2S crews also practised gunnery and bombing of a moving target – a shield towed by ships from Mikoszewo to Hel. Concrete LBC-50 practice bombs were used. In places where practice bombs, hit plumes of smoke were visible.

From 15 July-30 August 1952, due to refurbishment of Babie Doły air base, the 30th Naval Aviation Regiment with Tu-2S and Pe-2 aircraft of the Long Range Reconnaissance Squadron was deployed to Gdańsk-Wrzeszcz airfield. The Tu-2S aircraft of the Long Range Reconnaissance Squadron took part in the air parade, held on 29 June 1952 on Navy Day. Three crews made a flypast over the warships participating in the parade. As only a dozen or so aircraft took part in the parade, the three Tu-2S flew over the ships twice. The object was to make

[40]: *One of two Tu-2S aircraft operated by the Air Force Technical Institute served as the backdrop of a commemorative photograph.*

a propaganda impression of the power of the Naval Aviation, in truth very small in numbers.

An example of Polish reality of the 1950s is the use of a Tu-2S from the 30th Naval Aviation Regiment in pursuit of a fishing vessel, which was specified as naval aviation's special task in protection of the state border. On 28 August 1952 a Tu-2S crew was tasked with finding a fishing vessel, which had sailed out from Gdynia and had reportedly headed for Sweden. Having made the "searching manoeuvre" the crew found the vessel with its fishing net deployed far from the Polish coast. The aircraft overflew the fishing vessel and the crew identified the letters "GDY" in the vessel's hull number on its side. Then the pilot, overflying the vessel again, fired a burst from the two fixed 20 mm ShVAK cannons ahead of the vessel's bow. The vessel turned back and headed for the Polish coast. The Tu-2S repeatedly flew along the vessel's side on the same heading and rocking its wings showed the direction of the return to Gdynia. After the return to base the crew was ordered to fly again, this time with a bomb load. The bombs were to be a "strong warning argument" in case the vessel failed to return to the home port. The bomb-loaded aircraft searched for the fishing vessel, but failed to find it. Due to falling darkness the crew aborted the mission. Perhaps the fishing vessel returned to Gdynia in the meantime, but there was no confirmation. The Tu-2S, with a load of armed bombs (!), landed safely at Gdańsk-Wrzeszcz airfield. It was a precedent, because at that time the 30th Naval Aviation Regiment was not yet flying night missions on the Tu-2S aircraft. The crew was awarded a cita-

tion from the highest echelon and the aircraft commander was additionally rewarded with a camera.

In 1953 during exercises of Western ships in the Baltic Sea, the Long Range Reconnaissance Squadron held night alert duty of Tu-2S aircraft. Bombers with bomb loads and ammunition for machine guns and cannons were ready for quick take-off. Beginning in 1953, Tu-2S crews flew long missions on routes along the coast and over land. These aircraft simulated aerial targets for the air defence radar system, which was being developed at that time. Pairs of MiG-15 and Yak-23 were guided to intercept them. The Tu-2S crews called these sorties "radar station checks". The route of one such sortie led from Gdynia to Rozewie, then Świnoujście, Kostrzyn nad Odrą, Gorzów Wielkopolski, Bartoszyce and back to Gdynia. Tu-2S' range enabled such long missions. One such mission on 5 June 1953 lasted 3 hours and 15 minutes.

During tactical flying exercises, organized on division command level, a Tu-2S accidentally violated the airspace of the Soviet Union. The airplane with crew comprising Lt Henryk Jędrzejowski (pilot), Ens. Kazimierz Gawron (navigator) and Petty Officer Henryk Kuza (gunner/wireless operator) took off from Wrzeszcz airfield to simulate an "intruder" for fighters of a regiment based at Babie Doły. The Tu-2S flying over land at low altitude crossed the shoreline off Darłowo and, flying at an altitude of 200 m, reached the Bornholm area. There the aircraft headed east and climbed to 4,500 m. Flying east at that altitude the Tu-2S was to be intercepted by Polish fighters, guided by a ground command post. However, due to a navigational error, the aircraft reached the vicinity of Kuronian

Spit. Having noticed that it was not Vistula Spit, the crew turned left, heading for the open sea. There the Polish Tu-2S was intercepted by a pair of Soviet MiG-15 fighters. The MiG pilots rocked their wings, giving the crew of the Tu-2S (with large Polish checkerboards clearly visible) signs to follow them. Moreover, the wireless operator mixed up the colours of the identification flares he fired, adding further confusion. The Polish crew did not make use of this form of Polish-Soviet friendship and a forced visit to the base of the great ally. They descended and changed heading in a "friendly cloud", escaped the Soviet fighters and returned to base. It is possible that they managed to avoid being shot down. The crew admittedly succeeded in avoiding landing at a strange airfield, but failed to avoid long explanations before the Polish commanders and particularly the Soviet "advisors". The fate of the MiG pilots who lost the Polish aircraft is not known.

Crews of Tu-2S and Pe-2 aircraft from the 30th Naval Aviation Regiment practised aerial gunnery, firing at a target drogue towed by a Tu-2S. A Tu-2S pilot could the fire 20 mm ShVAK cannons mounted in the wing roots. He aimed by manoeuvring the entire aircraft in a shallow dive. Firing the ShVAK cannons was practised rather rarely. More often navigators and gunners

[41]: *The UTu-2 "8" as it was donated to the Polish Army Museum in Warsaw after having finished its service in the Air Force Technical Institute.*

[42]: *The UTu-2 preserved in the Polish Army Museum, with visible signs of deterioration. The number "8" is lacking and the checkerboards are of different style and size than the previous, original, ones. The spinners were repainted red, without retaining the previous colours.*

fired 12.7 mm UBT machine guns from their positions. They fired usually from one side to avoid hitting their own aircraft when turning the loaded gun from one side to another. There were cases of shooting off the wire antenna stretched between the antenna mast over the cockpit and the vertical stabilizer. One Tu-2S was adapted for target towing. A drum with reeled towing line was fitted to the bulkhead in the lower part of the gunner/wireless operator compartment. A rolled target drogue, attached to the end of the towing line, was suspended on an ejector in the bomb bay. The drum's RPM was slowed down after releasing the drogue by the gunner/wireless operator with the hydraulic brake installed in his compartment. On the pilot's command the navigator released the drogue from the ejector in the bomb bay, like a bomb. The gunner/wireless operator released slowly the hydraulic brake and unreeled the line with the drogue to a safe length of several hundred meters behind the tug aircraft. After the completion of the gunnery exercise the drogue was jettisoned over the airfield and exercise results were evaluated in the presence of the aircrews. Sometimes the drogue could not be jettisoned over the base because it had been shot off during the exercise. Each crew had their aircraft's guns loaded with ammunition with bullet tips painted in various colours. Thus the bullet holes on the target drogue had the colour of the bullets that had hit.

An accident occurred during a target towing sortie by a Tu-2S on 14 July 1953. The crew comprised Lt Henryk Jędrzejowski (pilot), LTJG Kazimierz Gawron (navigator) and CWO Alfred Szydowski (gunner/wireless operator). When all scheduled crews completed the exercise the pilot headed for Babie Doły air base to jettison the target drogue. Due to the length of the line, the drogue was well below the tug

aircraft. The aircraft descended to jettison the drogue from an altitude of about 50 m. The drogue was jettisoned after the towing line had been completely unreeled. The gunner/wireless operator usually slowed down the drum's rotation speed with the hydraulic brake so that the drogue fell at the runway threshold and the towing line on the grass, along the runway. However on that day, fearing that jettisoning of the drogue might be too late, off the airfield, he released the brake completely. As result a loop of steel line was made on the drum, spinning with excessive speed, and cut the gunner's flying helmet, suit and boots, causing numerous injuries. Other injuries were caused by numerous steel needles from the severed steel line. CWO Alfred Szydowski recovered after hospital treatment.

In 1954 Tu-2S crews commenced night flying training. It was a new element of training in the 30th Naval Aviation Regiment. First, the division's and regiment's command staff personnel commenced night training sorties in the UTu-2 and UIł-10. Initially only the flying technique was exercised. Then night flights in the traffic pattern and in manoeuvring came. For the duration of the exercises the aircraft were redeployed from Gdańsk-Wrzeszcz to Gdynia-Babie Doły airfield, which had elaborate radio navigation equipment for MiG-15 fighters.

During the service of Tu-2S aircraft in the 30th Naval Aviation Regiment two accidents took place. The first one occurred in April 1954. During take-off from Babie Doły air base the Tu-2S "2", piloted by LTJG Adam Michałek with instructor Lcdr Mikhail Cherdantsev (a Soviet officer), the starboard main wheel tyre blew and the aircraft veered off the runway. The strut of the damaged wheel was stuck in the hole of a runway lamp. The nose glazing and ARK-5 ADF receiver

[43]: *The Tu-2S "3" of the 19. LEH at Świdwin air base. The winch drum is visible beneath the fuselage. Lower tailfin sections and spinners are red. This aircraft was operated by the 19. LEH during 1954–1959.*

43

[44-45]: Tu-2S "3" at Świdwin air base in 1957. The flight engineer, 2nd Lt Mieczysław Kowalczuk, poses beside the aircraft.

[46]: *Open cockpit, occupied by the pilot and navigator. Large part of navigational equipment behind pilot's seat is visible. 2nd Lt Mieczysław Kowalczuk poses in the pilot's seat. Świdwin, 1957.*

were destroyed. This wasted many hours of arduous radio deviation correction on this aircraft. Such operation always required checking the radio deviation on 24 compass points, which meant turning the heavy aircraft and positioning it on that number of headings. At least ten soldiers were engaged in this task. During such operations the homing beacon had to be on, because the ADF had to be homed on its mast, which was not always visible. The damaged Tu-2S "2" was repaired and returned to service.

The modest inventory of Tu-2S aircraft meant that the only UTu-2 was used not only for flying technique checks. On the UTu-2 other flights, not related to bombing, were also made. It was used for cross-country flights and monitoring the radar coverage of the coastal area. During such sorties the instructor's position, fitted with flight controls but lacking the OPB-1D bombsight, was occupied by the navigator.

To supplement the Tu-2S aircraft in the Long Range Reconnaissance Squadron of the 30th Naval Aviation Regiment, the Tu-2S "5" was transferred from the Sochaczew-based 21. PLZ.

The second accident in the 30th Naval Aviation Regiment occurred on 29 March 1955. The Tu-2S "1", piloted by LTJG Adam Michałek, flew into a blizzard enroute from Malbork to Gdynia. The pilot decided to make an emergency landing near Izbica on frozen marshland. The weather soon became warmer and the aircraft began to sink into the melting swamp. There was no other way to recover it than to break it up for spare parts for other Tu-2S aircraft.

In the autumn of 1955 the UTu-2 "8" and Tu-2S "5" ended their service in the 30th Naval Aviation Regiment. Both were transferred to the 19th Tow Target Squadron *(19. LEH)* based at Słupsk. The Tu-2S were the last piston-powered bombers operated by the Polish Air Force after the Second World War. In 1956 the Long Range Reconnaissance Squadron of the 30th Naval Aviation Regiment was re-formed into 15th Independent Naval Aviation Reconnaissance Squadron (15. *Samodzielna Eskadra Lotnictwa Rozpoznawczego MW*), equipped with Il-28 and Il-28R aircraft.

Objective assessments of the handling qualities of the Tu-2S expressed by Polish airmen flying these bombers were published as late as the 1990s, free from propaganda glorifying and exaggerating the value of Soviet-made equipment. The most comprehensive review, expressed with hindsight, was made by Capt. Kazimierz Gawron, who flew the Tu-2S and Pe-2 bombers as navigator in the Long Range Reconnaissance Squadron of the 30th Naval Aviation Regiment, in his memoirs, published in 1996. He logged 91 sorties in Tu-2S and UTu-2 aircraft. The Tu-2S, operated as bomber and reconnaissance aircraft in Polish naval aviation, was ill-suited for long range reconnaissance duties. They were not fitted with specialized reconnaissance equipment, only with cameras. These were tactical bombers, intended for supporting ground troops by bombing fixed and mobile targets in enemy territory, close to the frontline. Two Tu-2S and one UTu-2 aircraft, assigned to the 30th Naval Aviation Regiment, were more advanced, safer

[47]: *Posing in the winch operator compartment of the Tu-2S "5" of the 19. LEH are the flight engineer, Cpl Józef Szwarc and crew chief, PFC Tadeusz Czubak. The blade antenna, visible in front of the compartment, distinguished this aircraft from "3" and "8".*

and more crew-friendly in comparison with weary Pe-2 bombers, also operated by the unit. Comparing both aircraft, the airmen compared the Tu-2S to a Polish FIAT 125p car and the Pe-2 to a crude Polish Syrena car. The pilot could master this aircraft after a dozen or so sorties. The Tu-2S, powered by two ASh-82FN radial engines rated at 1,850 hp each, could safely fly on one engine, while engine failure in a Pe-2 did not allow single-engined flight and usually meant a forced landing, which often resulted in a crash. The Tu-2S met aircrew requirements when it was entering the inventory of the 7th Bomber Aviation Regiment and the Long Range Reconnaissance Squadron of the 30th Naval Aviation Regiment, among others, because it was more comfortable and advanced than the weary and unreliable Pe-2. Thus flying them was perceived as an honour. Its flying and handling qualities were appreciated. According to Capt. Gawron: *"Apart from being easy to fly, the Tu-2S, larger and heavier than the Pe-2, was also safer – it was not as sensitive to every move the pilot made and was tolerant of possible errors. It was faster and had more powerful engines, which, combined with larger wing area, provided better flight safety. Landing the Tu-2S was easier than in the lighter Pe-2, featuring very strong, elastic landing gear. The Tu-2S was fitted with a de-icing system, comprising alcohol sprayers on the windscreen and propeller blades and pneumatic rubber de-icing boots on the wing leading edges. This allowed dispersion of any ice layer, sometimes rapidly building up when flying in clouds. There was no such system on the Pe-2 – there was a crash hazard."* According to the crews, flying

the Tu-2S was a pleasure. The Tu-2S, fitted with ARK-5 ADF, was capable of daytime cross-country flying in poor visibility and night flying (no such flights were made on the Pe-2). The Tu-2S provided better working conditions for the pilot and navigator, in more a spacious cockpit with better visibility.

The pilot and navigator's canopy was of the clamshell type, comprising two panels. The upper panel hinged to port and the lower two-section panel hinged to starboard. The crew embarked using the fold-down step in the lower fuselage on the starboard side and three rectangular kick-in steps above it. Three similar spring-loaded hand grips were situated on the spine. An anti-slip walkway ran along the fuselage on the upper area of the starboard wing and a dished hand grip was situated on the trailing edge of the starboard wing at the fuselage. According to Capt. Gawron the pilots and navigators in naval uniforms did not use these steps and grips, but climbed a three-section ladder, folding to one side, positioned at the trailing edge of the starboard wing. Capt Gawron described a situation when his pilot, LTJG Edward Mataczun, did not wait for the mechanic to set up the ladder behind the wing but did it himself instead. The ladder, positioned incorrectly, collapsed under the pilot with his parachute. As result, LTJG Mataczun fell from a two metre height onto the concrete apron, but was not hurt. This pilot was famous for his swearing talent and on this occasion he uttered a particularly elaborate volley of abuse. Also Col. Kazimierz Wierzbicki, recollecting preparations for the 1 May parade with the use of all Tu-2S aircraft, deployed then to Kroczewo airfield, mentioned that all Tu-2S crews also used ladders there. Perhaps Polish crews considered this way of climbing the wing more comfortable than using the factory-fitted steps and grips in the fuselage. It is hard to imagine disembarking after a flight. Descending backwards down the wing and finding the kick-in steps in the fuselage skin was not easy. Folding down the lower step from the cockpit was not possible and the required assistance of the ground crew, who probably would help the crewmembers to disembark without using the ladder.

The cockpit also provided good downward visibility for the pilot and navigator, through the asymmetrically glazed lower nose section. The pilot was protected by 15 mm armour plate and his seat was offset 120 mm to the aircraft's longitudinal axis. The navigator did not have his own seat. He sat on his parachute in the floor recess, shaped to accommodate the parachute. Sitting behind the pilot, slightly to the right, he also had good visibility through the starboard section of the nose glazing. The instrument panel consisted of three segments, arranged so that some of the instruments could be controlled by the pilot,

[48]: *UTu-2 "8" during engine run-up on the grass part of the Świdwin air base. In the* 19. LEH *this aircraft was used to simulate a target for artillery or ground-controlled interception (GCI) radars.*

[49]: *The crew in front of UTu-2 "8". Left to right: 1st Lt Stanisław Widawski (pilot), 2nd Lt Eugeniusz Politowicz (flight engineer) and 2nd Lt Bronisław Grzywnowicz (navigator). This aircraft was not equipped with the target towing winch.*

some could be easily read by the navigator and the rest of the instrument panel was visible for both crewmembers. To fire the machine gun the navigator with parachute could easily change position, turning back, which was much more difficult in the Pe-2. The navigator, in contrast to the pilot, usually did not strap into the cockpit, which could result in injuries. Such a situation which occurred in 1953 was recalled by Capt. Gawron. A MiG-15 piloted by LTJG Bronisław Siwy of the 34th Naval Aviation Fighter Regiment (34. *Pułk Lotnictwa Myśliwskiego Marynarki Wojennej – 34. PLM MW)* flew across the nose of a Tu-2S piloted by the CO of the 30th Naval Aviation Regiment *(30. PL MW)*, Capt Mikhail Cherdantsev. To avoid collision the bomber pilot pushed violently on the control column, throwing the aircraft into a steep dive. There was no collision, but the g force threw the unstrapped navigator, with parachute, onto the upper panel of the canopy. When the pilot pulled on the yoke, the navigator was pressed into the seat. With this ridiculous stunt the "valiant" MiG-15 pilot wanted to scare the Tu-2S crew. He heard one, very rude, Russian word uttered by the bomber pilot.

In the Tu-2S the navigator operated the 12.7 mm machine gun, firing it from a kneeling position. The ammunition box could contain 170 rounds, but for practice firing at a target drogue only 30 rounds were loaded. In the 30th Naval Aviation Regiment only a few times was the number of the rounds loaded increased to 40. So-called "double" exercises were made then. There were actually fewer rounds than needed for double gunnery exercises because the expended case bags could not hold more expended cases and links. During so-called "continuous firing" the expended case bag could be ripped apart. Cases and links spilled into the cockpit could jam the control cables, seizing the flight controls.

The opinion of Captain Gawron, who flew Tu-2S and UTu-2 in the 30th Naval Aviation Regiment, about the utility of these aircraft in the Naval Aviation classified as reconnaissance bombers, is objective and realistic. *"Due to limited tactical capabilities and poor armament they were not intended for anti-shipping operations. They lacked reconnaissance equipment and armament sitable for maritime combat aircraft, such as torpedoes or mines. The Tu-2S aircraft operated during the Cold War in terms of equipment were inferior to enemy aircraft. Used as reconnaissance aircraft, they were not equipped with radar to enable long-range reconnaissance at sea, in bad weather and at night. They were unsuitable for basic tasks of the naval aviation. The probability of hitting maritime targets during level bombing was small, besides these aircraft were not capable of defending themselves against the ships' anti-aircraft weapons. There was no crew training in this field at all. The gun armament (20 mm cannons and 12.7 mm machine guns) enabled engaging only small vessels."* Here are a few sentences written by a navigator of "those years": *"We were not informed about these facts, instead we were persuaded to believe that we fly the world's best aircraft and we should be proud of it… We were maritime aviation only by name, due to operational control, without possibility of performing tasks typical for it."*

[50]: *Airmen of the 19. LEH* standing next to the tail of the UTu-2 "8". Left to right: *2nd Lt Władysław Stępniak (flight engineer), 1st Lt Zbigniew Turosz (pilot) and two enlisted groundcrew.*

Colors and markings of Polish Tu-2S aircraft

Tu-2S aircraft, tail numbers "5" and "7", operated by the 7th Dive Bomber Regiment (7. PBN), based at Ławica wore initially, and even as late as 1950 the post-war Soviet camouflage. Upper surfaces of the wings, engine nacelles and fuselage, fuselage sides and tailfins were painted in dark grey and blue grey disruptive pattern, in accordance with No. 2 scheme from the painting instruction. (No. 1 scheme, also concerning two-tone camouflage of upper and side surfaces, but with more elaborate, denser pattern of streaked splotches was not applied on Polish aircraft). Surfaces visible from below were light blue. Lower parts of the external surfaces of the tailfins and spinners were red – which denoted the assignment to the 7. PBN. It is not known whether only these two aircraft wore the dark grey/blue grey camouflage. Perhaps some other Tu-2S, "3", "4" or "6", wore a similar disruptive paint scheme. Probably the Tu-2S "1", "2" and UTu-2 "8", received in October 1949 from a Soviet air unit based at Legnica, already had olive green upper and side surfaces. The spinners were probably dark red.

It is a known fact that the aircraft transferred from the 7. PBN to the 30. PL MW in 1950 had olive green upper and side surfaces. It can be assumed that after only one year of service they did not need repainting and commenced service at sea in their previous colours. There are few photographs taken in the early period of service of the Tu-2S aircraft in Poland and it is impossible to determine how many aircraft wore the post-war dark grey/blue grey Soviet camouflage. Later in their service the aircraft had upper and side surfaces painted olive green. Lower surfaces were light blue. The shades of these colours changed after overhauls. De-icing boots on the leading edges of the wing and horizontal stabilizer were dark grey. White single-digit tail numbers were painted on the tailfins. On three aircraft, operated by the 30. PL MW from 1950, the numbers "1", "2" and "8" were painted on the inner surfaces of the tailfins. In the Air Force units the numbers were painted on the outer surfaces. The checkerboards were painted on lower wing surfaces, fuselage and tailfins. On the tailfins they were painted so that one half was on the rudder and the other on the vertical stabilizer. Aircraft of the 30. PL MW had the spinner tips and lower sections of the tailfins painted white. The UTu-2 "8", transferred from the Air Force Technical Institute to the Polish Army Museum in Warsaw, arrived there with two-colour spinners. The spinner tips were red. After having been repainted at the museum it had the entire spinners painted red and smaller checkerboards. The wheel rims were painted green.

[51]: A photograph from the aircraft exhibition, held at Warsaw-Okęcie airfield during 26 August-9 September 1956. Of interest is the background with part of the Tu-2S (ex "5") without the tail number. Two ejection seat guide rails protruding from the ejection seat test bed are visible. In the foreground is An-2, s/n 16311 (of Soviet production), operated by the 36th Special Duty Independent Aviation Regiment, delivered on 22 June 1956.

[52]: The Tu-2S (ex "5") without tail number, displayed at the 1956 Okęcie exhibition is visible in the background, positioned behind the Lim-2 "1903", assigned to the 1. Fighter Aviation Regiment "Warsaw" from 13 August 1956.

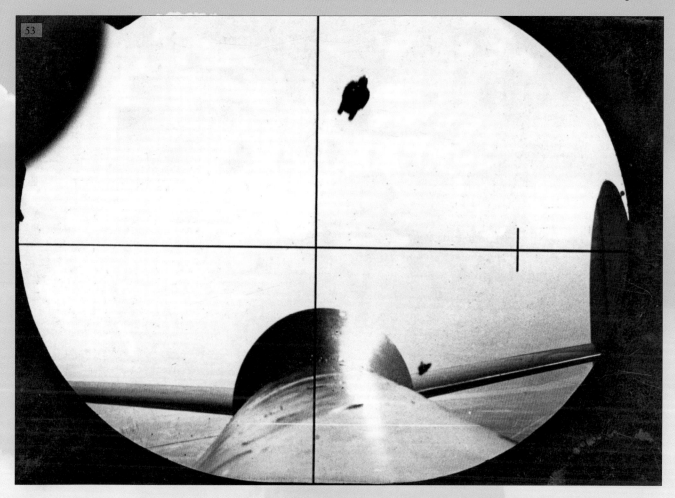

[53-55]: A sequence of three
photographs, document-
ing the ejection of Capt.
Tadeusz Dulla from the Tu-2S
(ex "5") in 1956.

[56]: *Tu-2S "5" of the 3rd Squadron, 7th Dive Bomber Regiment, Poznań-Ławica, 1950. Upper and side surfaces are painted in a disruptive pattern, consisting of blue grey (AMT-11) and dark grey (AMT-12). Lower surfaces are light blue.*

[57]: *One of the first photographs of the Tu-2S "5" and probably "7", taken at Ławica airfield in the summer of 1950. Both aircraft wear post-war Soviet camouflage, with upper and side surfaces of the fuselage and wings painted in dark grey and blue grey patches. Lower surfaces were light blue. Visible on "5", elements painted blue grey by the scheme No. 2 are the starboard tailfin, port rudder and fuselage side. In dark grey are the rear section of the starboard engine cowling, upper side of the fuselage from the horizontal stabilizer to the gunner/wireless operator compartment and the port vertical stabilizer.*

[58]: *Camouflage pattern on the Tu-2S "5". The disruptive pattern of blue grey (AMT-11) and dark grey (AMT-12) is similar to the scheme No. 2 in the aircraft's painting instruction. The spinner tips are red. The propeller blades are black with yellow tips.*

58

[59]: Tu-2S "7" of the 3rd Squadron, 7th Dive Bomber Regiment, Poznań-Ławica, summer of 1950. Upper and side surfaces are painted in a disruptive pattern, consisting of blue grey (AMT-11) and dark grey (AMT-12). Lower surfaces are light blue. Red spinner tips and lower tailfin section are regiment identification markings. The number "7" is white.

59

[60]: Tu-2S "7" of the 7th Dive Bomber Regiment, based at Poznań-Ławica until October 1950. The aircraft wears original post-war Soviet camouflage. Upper and side surfaces are painted in a disruptive pattern of blue grey and dark grey. Lower surfaces are light blue. Blue grey fragments of the airplane are the upper starboard cowling section, rear section of the starboard spinner, aft fuselage side outer tailfin surface. Dark grey elements visible in the photograph are the upper fuselage surface with the canopy frame, upper fuselage above the aft window, rear section of the port spinner, visible fragment of the port engine nacelle and aft section of the starboard nacelle. Characteristic different colours of the rear spinner sections and aforementioned colour scheme details result from the use of No. 2 variant of the aircraft painting instruction. Red spinner tips and lower tailfin section are regiment identification markings. The number "7" is white.

60

[61]: Tupolev Tu-2S "1" of the Long Range Reconnaissance Squadron, 30th Naval Aviation Regiment, Gdańsk-Wrzeszcz 1955. The aircraft wears a paint scheme of olive green upper and light blue lower surfaces. White spinner tips and white lower tailfin sections are the identification markings of the 30th Naval Aviation Regiment. White number "1" was painted on the inner tailfin surfaces.

[62]: Tu-2S "1" of the 30th Naval Aviation Regiment, damaged during a forced landing on frozen marshland near Łeba on 29 March 1955. The aircraft did not return to service. It was dismantled on the spot and its components were used as spare parts for other Tu-2S aircraft in service.

[63]: *Tupolev Tu-2S "2" of the Long Range Reconnaissance Squadron, 30th Naval Aviation Regiment, Gdynia-Babie Doły 1954. Upper and side surfaces are olive green and lower surfaces are light blue.*

63

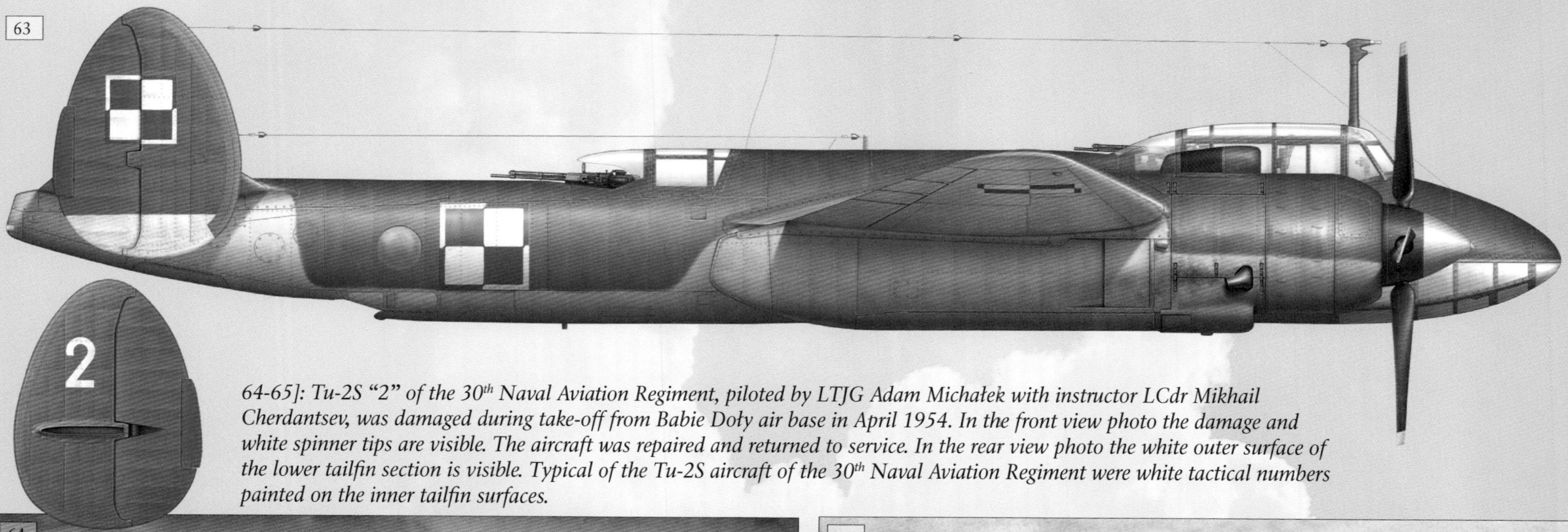

64-65]: *Tu-2S "2" of the 30th Naval Aviation Regiment, piloted by LTJG Adam Michałek with instructor LCdr Mikhail Cherdantsev, was damaged during take-off from Babie Doły air base in April 1954. In the front view photo the damage and white spinner tips are visible. The aircraft was repaired and returned to service. In the rear view photo the white outer surface of the lower tailfin section is visible. Typical of the Tu-2S aircraft of the 30th Naval Aviation Regiment were white tactical numbers painted on the inner tailfin surfaces.*

65

64

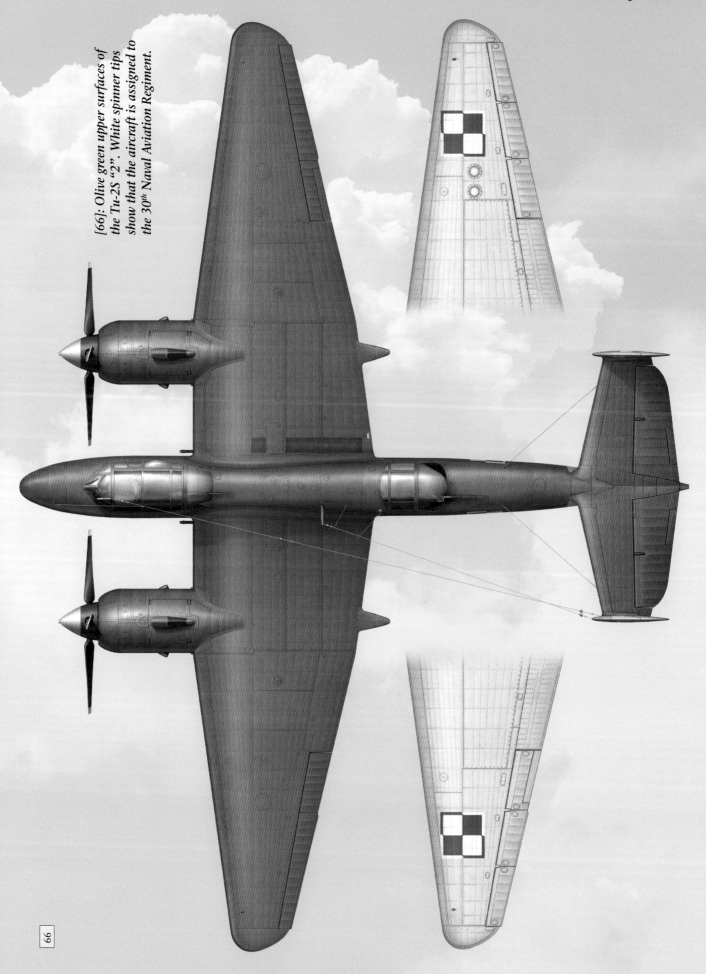

[66]: Olive green upper surfaces of the Tu-2S "2". White spinner tips show that the aircraft is assigned to the 30th Naval Aviation Regiment.

66

[67]: *Tupolev Tu-2S "3" of the 19th Tow Target Squadron (19. LEH), based at Świdwin. The aircraft was operated by 19. LEH during 1954-1959 in olive green and light blue paint scheme. Lower tailfin sections and spinner tips are red.*

[68]: *Ventral gunner position, modified to accommodate the winch drum for the target drogue towing line. This is the first version of the modification of the Tu-2S "3" for target towing duties. Later an improved drum was mounted just aft of the glazing frame and the glazing was faired over with sheet metal. A navigator, 2nd Lt Bronisław Firganek, poses beside the aircraft.*

[69]: *Tupolev Tu-2S "5" during its service in the 35. PLB and 21. PLZ. Red spinner tips and lower tailfin sections are markings retained from the period of the aircraft's service in the 7. PLB.*

[70]: *Tu-2S "5" in two-tone camouflage, displayed in public with gun armament (probably during its service in the 35. PLB or 21. PLZ). Note the reversed checkerboard visible on the lower wing surface, red spinner tips and lower tailfin sections. On the left part of LWD "Żuraw" SP-GLB is visible in the background.*

[71]: *Tu-2S "5", armed with 12.7 mm machine guns in the navigator and gunner/wireless operator positions. Red lower tailfin section below the number "5" is visible. The Il-28 "3" and An-2 aircraft are interesting, similar to the positioning of the aircraft during the exhibition at Okęcie airfield in 1956. The Tu-2S ex "5" was then displayed after the end of its service in the 19. LEH and conversion of the winch operator compartment into an ejection seat testbed. The "ex 5" displayed then had no tail number and red tailfin markings and the checkerboard on the wing was painted correctly.*

43

[72]: Tupolev Tu-2S "5" of the 19th Tow Target Squadron (19. LEH), based at Świdwin in 1955. The aircraft wears two-tone paint scheme and has the later variant of the winch drum installation, aft of the ventral gunner position glazing frame. The checkerboard on the fuselage is painted close to the window. The spinner is red. The white number 5 is stencilled without filling the gaps.

[73]: The Tu-2S "5" of the 19. LEH had an additional blade antenna in front of the winch operator compartment. It was operated by the 19. LEH from the autumn of 1955 until it was struck off the squadron's inventory in the first half of 1956.

[74]: *Tupolev Tu-2S "5" during its service in the Air Force Technical Institute in 1956. After the overhaul the aircraft had the two-tone paint scheme applied again. Spinner tips were painted red. In place of the winch operator compartment a test bed for ejection seats was installed.*

[76]: *A frame from a film tape showing part of the Tu-2S of the Air Force Technical Institute. The moment of the successful ejection of Capt. Tadeusz Dulla in an ejection seat from the modified gunner/wireless operator compartment was recorded.*

[75]: *A photograph of the Tu-2S "ex 5 – ejection seat test bed", described as taken during the exhibition at Okęcie airfield in 1956. Note the lack of the number "5" on the tailfin and red lower tailfin sections and correct colour sequence of the checkerboard on the wing.*

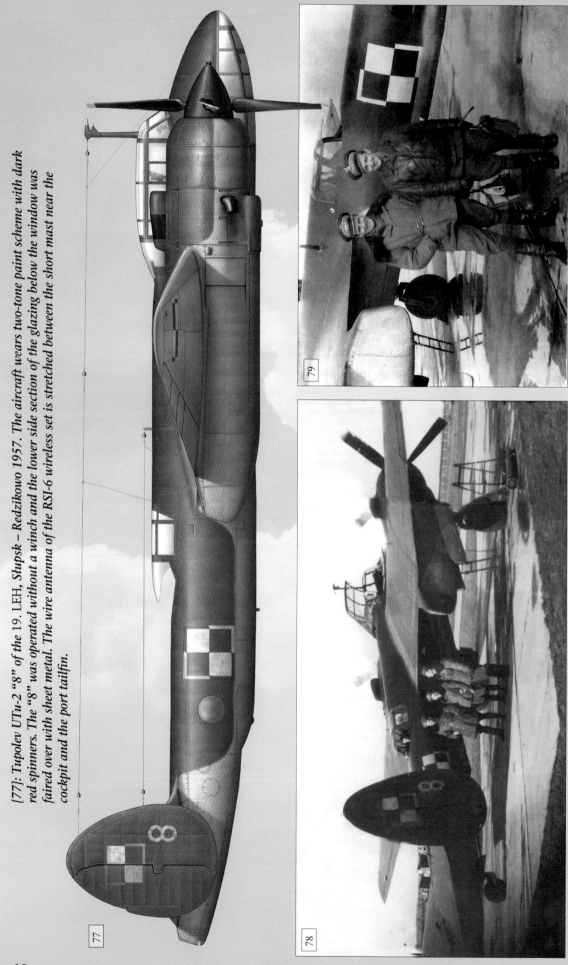

[77]

[78]

[79]

[77]: Tupolev UTu-2 "8" of the 19. LEH, Słupsk – Redzikowo 1957. The aircraft wears two-tone paint scheme with dark red spinners. The "8" was operated without a winch and the lower side section of the glazing below the window was faired over with sheet metal. The wire antenna of the RSI-6 wireless set is stretched between the short mast near the cockpit and the port tailfin.

[78]: UTu-2 at Świdwin air base. The aircraft has no winch drum beneath the fuselage. Wire antenna of RSI-6 wireless set is visible next to the tailfin and its short mast on the fuselage. Note flaking paint on the checkerboard and number and weary paint finish.

[79]: A pilot, 1st Lt Tadeusz Starzyński (left) and navigator, 2nd Lt Bronisław Firganek, stand beside the UTu-2 "8" of the 19. LEH. In "8" the permanently open aft compartment, without the machine gun mount, was occupied by the flight engineer. On top it was covered with a fixed roof pressed from a single Plexiglas sheet. Access to the compartment and bailout was through the side glazed canopy section, hinging to port. The upper canopy section hinged to starboard and was jettisoned in case of emergency. On the left, ahead of the compartment, a short mast of the wire antenna of the RSI-6 wireless set and antenna inlet are visible.

[80]: *Tupolev UTu-2 "8", operated by the Air Force Technical Institute, Warsaw-Bemowo airfield, 1958. The aircraft wears olive green/light blue paint scheme, refreshed during the last overhaul in the Aviation Repair Works No. 2, with red spinner tips and white number "8".*

[81]: *A photograph of the UTu-2 "8", operated by the Air Force Technical Institute, taken by Janusz Szymański at Warsaw-Bemowo airfield, which "for the purpose of strategic deception" was named after a nearby locality – Babice. The aircraft had renewed paint finish with red spinner tips. On the lower surface of the wing (only the port one) two retractable landing lights are visible.*

[82]: *Tarpaulin-covered UTu-2 "8" of the Air Force Technical Institute, photographed by Janusz Szymański at Warsaw-Bemowo airfield, next to a Lim-5 fighter. Inner surfaces of lower tailfin sections are blue. The helicopter without number, visible behind the UTu-2, is a Mi-1, previously used by WSK Świdnik factory as production pattern for licence-built SM-1 helicopters.*

Sukhoi UTB-2

Sukhoi UTB-2 – trainer variant of the Tupolev Tu-2 bomber. The Tu-2S bomber, produced from 1943 on, had no trainer version for pilot conversion and training. Only after the end of the war, in February 1946, a decision was made to develop a trainer aircraft, with dimensions and flight characteristics similar to the bomber. Since the design bureau led by Andrei N. Tupolev was busy with the urgent task of building a copy of the Boeing B-29 bomber (called Tupolev Tu-4 in the USSR), the task of developing the trainer version of the Tu-2S bomber was given to the design team led by Pavel O. Sukhoi. The design of this aircraft, named UTB-2 (abbreviation of Russian *uchebno – trenirovochnyi bombardirovshchik* – bomber trainer) included features to let it attain the following performance figures: maximum speed 375 km/h at an altitude of 200 m, landing speed

[83-85]: A unique series of air-to-air photographs of UTB-2 aircraft in flight near Dęblin at an altitude of 400 m in May 1950. The aircraft had early markings S-4 and S-7, later replaced with two-digit numbers. The spinner tips are white and red.

115 km/h, maximum altitude 6,000 m, range 800 km, time of climb to 3,000 m – 11 minutes. Capability of carrying a 200 kg bomb load on external hardpoints was stipulated. The objective of the work commenced in 1946 was to develop an easy to fly and maintain, economical aircraft for bomber crew training. Modified for training purposes, dual control versions of combat aircraft, such as the USB (trainer variant of the SB-2) bomber, then still service in small numbers, were obsolete and weary and in turn the UPe-2 aircraft were costly in operation and difficult to fly, which made pilot training on these aircraft longer. Therefore it was decided to develop and use in training an aircraft easy to fly. Only after having mastered this aircraft would the trainee convert directly to a combat aircraft or a dual control version of a combat aircraft. To accelerate the design process of the new trainer aircraft, the airframe of a production Tu-2S

that the Sukhoi facility received in March 1946 was partially redesigned. Its wings and rear fuselage, with the tail section, were adopted. A new forward fuselage section with widened and lengthened cockpit was designed. The cockpit housed two seats for the instructor and trainee, arranged side-by-side, with the navigator's seat behind them. Depending on the training needs, these seats could be occupied by a pilot, navigator and navigator trainee. The navigator's seat and equipment was behind the pilot seats. The navigator sat with his back to the direction of flight, on a folding round seat similar to the seat mounted in the gunner's compartment. In contrast with the Tu-2, the cockpit had no hinged upper and side panels. The crew boarded the aircraft through the ventral hatch, opening downwards. The upper section of the canopy was jettisoned in emergency to enable the crew to bail out. The bomb bay

[86]: *Rear fuselage with tailfin of an UTB-2 marked with the letter S at Dęblin air base in winter, early 1950s.*

[87]: *Report before a sortie in an UTB-2 at Dęblin air base. Racks for 50-100 kg practice bombs are visible beneath the fuselage. The hub of two-blade VISh-11V propeller is covered with white and red tipped spinner.*

[88]: The instructor and trainee in the cockpit of an UTB-2, photographed from the navigator's position. The trainee's seat on the left is occupied by officer cadet Jerzy Wójcik, who in 1963 with the rank of Major was appointed commander of the 33. PLB and in 1966 led the "Eagle" parade formation.

[89]: Another photograph of a UTB-2 cockpit with the crew in flight. The instructor's seat on the right is occupied by Sergeant-Officer Cadet Zdzisław Szczucki, nicknamed "Bambo" by his colleagues due to his dark complexion. In 1956, in the rank of Captain, he was appointed commander of the 35. PLB.

and two 20 mm cannons in the wing roots, fired by the pilot, were removed. The navigator's machine gun mount and ventral gunner position were also removed. In place of the previous gunner/wireless operator position a similar VUB-68 gun mount for gunner training was retained. The gun armament comprised a single UBT machine gun with 60 rounds of ammunition. In the fuselage there was a passage from the cockpit to the gunner's compartment. Beneath the central fuselage, in place of the removed bomb bay, external racks for four 50 kg or 100 kg practice bombs were installed. The aforementioned changes reduced the weight by 4,000 kg in comparison with the Tu-2S. This allowed use of less powerful engines, more economical because they worked on cheaper fuel of lower octane number. In redesigned, narrower nacelles Ash-21 radial engines, rated at 700 hp (514.5 kW) and WISh-IIV two-blade propellers, known from Yak-11 single-seat trainers, were installed. New engine mounts shifted the engines forward by 150 mm to maintain the c-of-g. Lighter, single strut landing gear with wheels of smaller diameter was also adopted. The main wheels had the dimensions 900 x 300 mm and the tailwheel 440 x 210 mm. The prototype of the UTB-2 first flew on 14 June 1946. After the state evaluation necessary improvements were introduced. Series production was launched in 1947 at Factory No. 381 in Moscow. The first production aircraft, serial number 3810101 (in the serial number 381 denoted the factory, 01 the number of production batch and 01 the number of the aircraft within the batch), was completed in early May 1947. This aircraft had a fuselage 300 mm longer. To improve stability, the engines were shifted 150 mm forward. The characteristic feature of the nose section, from the prototype to the last production example of the UTB-2, was the asymmetry of the lower glazing panels. (The only drawings of the UTB-2, made by N. Gordyukov, published in the 1970s in "Modellist Konstruktor" and copied in Czechoslovakia and Poland erroneously show the forward view of the nose section with symmetric glazing). During the production run the UTB-2, like the Tu-2S, began to be equipped with RPKO-10M direction finder and RV-2 radar altimeter. During 1947-1949 a total of 176 UTB-2 aircraft were produced with the use of Tu-2S components. The prototype of a dive bomber trainer version UTB-2P (P for *pikiruyushchiy*) with air brakes under the wings did not enter production. In 1948 a few aircraft intended for low-level torpedo attack practice were built for the naval aviation. They were designated UTB-2T (T for *torpedonosyets*). Production of UTB-2 bomber trainers was terminated in 1949, because the Factory No. 381 commenced production of MiG-15 fighters, demand for which increased after the outbreak of the Korean War.

Shortly after the delivery of eight Tu-2S aircraft, UTB-2 trainers were also delivered to this regiment. These aircraft had excellent flight characteristics, enabling quick pilot training. The exact date of their delivery to Poland is difficult to determine. On 7 October 1949 five aircraft of this type entered the inventory, serial numbers: 3811804, 3811805, 3811806, 3711807 and 3811810. In contrast with the Tu-2S aircraft, these were new from the factory. They came from the last, 18th production batch, produced in May 1949. After re-equipping of the 7. PBN with Tu-2S aircraft, planned for early 1950, a detailed program of air and ground crew training was developed. According to this program it was intended to con-

[90]: *The cockpit of a UTB-2. The trainee sits on the left and the instructor on the right. The antenna mast was fitted to the star-board section of the canopy. Typical for the Tu-2 air thermometer and pitot-static tube for the airspeed indicator, vertical speed indicator and altimeter are mounted atop the mast. The upper section of the canopy could be jettisoned in emergency to enable the crew to bail out.*

[91]: *Refueling of a UTB-2 aircraft. The Schrenk-type flap is slightly lowered. Standing on the wing and supervising the refueling is the commander of the 1ˢᵗ Bomber Pilot Training Squadron of the Officer Flying Training School at Dęblin. A three-segment ladder leaning against the wing was also used in maintenance of the Tu-2S aircraft.*

[92]: *Instructor's remarks for officer cadets before a training sortie in the UTB-2 "26".*

[93]: *UTB-2 aircraft with tactical numbers 23, 25 and 24 prepared for training sorties of bomber crews in the Officer Flying Training School at Dęblin in 1954.*

[94]: *UTB-2 "23" taxiing with lowered flaps.*

duct intensive aircrew training during 16 March – 5 April on UTB-2 aircraft. It was assumed that every pilot would have to log 15-22 training sorties lasting in total 3-4 hours to master basic flying skills. Another 31–40 sorties, lasting in total 6-8 hours, were intended for further training and perfecting previously learned skills. Separate training was planned for ground crews, to prepare them to maintain the UTB-2 aircraft. From April to June 1950 further training on UTB-2 aircraft was conducted, during which 20 sorties, lasting a total 35 hours were flown. In the spring and summer the crews in training flew to the bombing range, where 30 practice bombings were conducted. After completion of full training program on the UTB-2, selected pilots were prepared to convert to the Tu-2S.

After the start of training on the Tu-2S bombers in the 7. PBN, four UTB-2 aircraft, 3811804, 3811805, 3811806 and 3711807, were transferred to Dęblin on 30 March 1950. They were assigned to the 2nd Training Squadron. The aircraft s/n 3811810 remained in the 7. PBN, where it was used for

training. In the spring of 1951 the 1st Bomber Pilot Training Squadron was formed in the Officer Flying Training School in Dęblin with four UTB-2s, 14 Pe-2 bombers and 11 UPe-2 trainer aircraft in its inventory. The squadron commander was Capt. Aleksander Milart. In the Dęblin school the UTB-2s replaced worn-out USB aircraft. These were modified SB-2 bombers of pre-war production. The USB had an open cockpit for the instructor, protected only with a windshield in the nose. In 1949 they were no longer used for pilot training because their technical condition did not allow it. Despite the fact that the UTB-2 aircraft were intended not only for pilot, but also for navigator and gunner training, in Dęblin only pilots were trained on them. For gunner and navigator training the Pe-2, Li-2 and Po-2 aircraft were used. The extensively used UTB-2 aircraft had a short time between overhauls and, with four in active service, two were always undergoing overhaul. UTB-2 overhauls were conducted by Aviation Repair Works no. 2 in Bydgoszcz, which also overhauled the Tu-2S. In Dęblin only

95   [95]: UTB-2 "25" before take-off. Dęblin 1954.

96   [96]: An UTB-2 just after liftoff.

[97]: *Warming-up of the Ash-21 engine at Dęblin airfield. The engine nacelle is covered with a quilted hood. The marking UTB-2 "27" is visible on the gasoline heater. On the lower surface of the port wing two folding landing lights are visible. The deflection angle of these light was adjusted electrically as in the Tu-2. Position in vertical and horizontal plane could be different for the inner and outer light. On the tailplane of the aircraft standing nearby only the right half of the checkerboard is visible. The other half was not painted – probably after a repair.*

Suhoi UTB-2 in Poland

Serial number	Known Tactical number
3810406	
3810605	
3811204	
3811603	
3811804	
3811805	
3811806	
3811807	
3811810	"20"

[98]: *A commemorative photograph taken at Dęblin in winter by the landing gear of a UTB-2. The wheel is covered with a tarpaulin and the engine nacelle is covered with a quilted hood*

minor repairs and engine changes were made. Unfortunately the ASh-21 engines of the UTB-2 aircraft were quite unreliable. In situations when engines failed, recovery was possible thanks to the excellent flight characteristics of these aircraft and skills of the flight instructors. The then sergeant-officer cadet Paweł Gawron, who was trained on these aircraft by Capt. Witold Białecki, remembered the excellent flight characteristics of the UTB-2.

When a pilot trained on the UTB-2 made an error, thanks to the exceptional flight characteristics of these aircraft the flight instructor could usually rescue the airplane and crew without great difficulties. Such a situation took place, among others in 1950, when an officer cadet was flying an UTB-2 with examining instructor, Maj. Petr Aleksiyenko (a Soviet officer). According to the account of this officer cadet, it was an examination flight, checking the trainee's skills before flying the first solo. The aircraft, approaching landing on one engine with flaps lowered, "floated" over the runway and the airfield turned out to be too short for the officer cadet. The UTB-2 began staggering in the air. Major Aleksiyenko increased the RPM of the idling engine and managed to make a go-around on full power of both engines. The engine simulating being inoperative before the landing had in fact the RPM reduced to idle and managed to attain full power in this critical situation. The scolding the officer cadet got after his flying error on approach was, according to him, "terrible". During training sorties when flying on one engine was practiced, the instructors never turned the other engine off, only reducing its power to idle to avoid the risk that the engine might not restart. The ASh-21 engines, which proved reliable as the Yak-11 powerplant, in UTB-2 worked in tougher conditions and often failed.

[99]: Crew of a UTB-2 posing for a photograph before a sortie in winter conditions.

[100]: Cockpit hatch with lowered three-step ladder.

To facilitate take-off the tailwheel was locked in the straight position with a wire, operated by a lever in the cockpit. After landing the pilot had to remember to unlock the wheel with the same lever. With the tailwheel locked the pilot could not turn when taxiing. Often the instructor had to remind the trainee of this necessary, but often forgotten, action.

Pilots trained on the UTB-2 in 1950 remember frequent remarks of instructors during taxi, take-off and landing roll to press the rudder pedals with the whole foot or preferably heel to deflect the rudder. Pressing the rudder pedals with just toes actuated the left or right main wheel brake, as in the Tu-2. Operating the brakes skillfully, the pilot could change the direction of the aircraft rolling on the runway or to the parking stand. Rapid or unintentional braking of one or especially two wheels posed the threat of damaging the aircraft in an accident.

Airmen who flew these aircraft mention the failure on 29 June 1951 as example of getting out of trouble in flight thanks to pilot skills, combined with excellent flight characteristics of the UTB-2. After a test flight after an engine change, during a low pass over the airfield at the altitude of 50 m one engine quit. When the pilot, Capt. Aleksander Milart, was making the turn to land the other engine also quit. The experienced pilot landed on a forest clearing at nearby Bonów bombing range. The aircraft stopped a few meters short of a high embankment. Despite this emergency landing with inoperative engines the aircraft was not severely damaged. It was hoisted, the landing

gear was lowered and it was stated then that only one engine had a failure. As result Capt. Milart was accused of a flying error. The place where Capt. Milart had landed was impossible to reach and evacuate the aircraft from. A provisional airstrip was prepared on the clearing. The aircraft was turned back in the direction from which it had landed. Maj. Petr Aleksiyenko, the deputy commandant of the Dęblin school and 1st Lt Aleksander Kwiatkowski, the commander of UTB-2 flight, took their places at the controls. The aircraft took off, but shortly after the liftoff one engine quit. The pilots hardly managed to make it to Dęblin and made an emergency landing across the runway without making a circuit. It turned out that both emergency landings were caused by damaged RS-2 mixture governors on both engines. Captain Milart, unjustly suspected of a pilot error, was apologized to by the school commandant, Col. Szczepan Ścibior.

From May 1950 to February 1951 two UTB-2 aircraft were operated by the 7th Bomber Aviation Regiment *(7. PLB)*, then based at Malbork. The other aircraft, borrowed from the Dęblin school at that time was 3811805. It turned out that one UTB-2 was not enough to provide necessary flight training in the *7. PLB.* Instrument flying was practiced most frequently. In July 1952 one flight in limited visibility, four flights in clouds and six flights in a hooded cockpit were logged. The borrowed 3811805 returned to the Dęblin school, which from 31 March 1951 had four aircraft of this type.

Between 20 and 24 March 1952 four UTB-2 aircraft were obtained from a Soviet bomber regiment. These were serial numbers 3810406 (produced in December 1947), 3810605 (produced in February 1948), 3811204 (produced in August 1948) and 3811603 (newest – produced in February 1949). These four aircraft entered the inventory of the 1st Squadron of the Dęblin school and were used for pilot training. The eight UTB-2 aircraft operated by the school had tactical numbers 21 through 29, painted on the fuselages. Despite eight UTB-2 aircraft in the school's inventory, only 4-6 aircraft were in operation at any one time. In December 1952 there were six UTB-2 aircraft in the school's inventory. In January 1953 these aircraft were operated by the 1st and 3rd Flight of the 1st Squadron of the Officer Flying Training School. In late 1953 the squadron had seven UTB-2 aircraft and one was being overhauled.

101

[101-102]: *Air-to-air photographs of UTB-2s with tactical numbers "24", "27" and "21", taken in winter scenery from the cockpit of a fourth airplane, near Dęblin.*

102

[103]: The UTB-2 "24" leading a formation. In contrast with other aircraft it has the number painted ahead of the checkerboard. Note the darker shade of the paint coating between the wing trailing edge and checkerboard.

[104]: Two officer cadets of Officer Flying Training School at Dęblin. Standing on the right is Kazimierz Gawron, who during 1950-1954 flew as navigator on Tu-2S and UTu-2 in the 30th Naval Aviation Regiment. Standing on the right is his brother Paweł during his flying training on UTB-2. Dęblin, May 1950.

During take-off on a training sortie on 15 January 1954 in UTB-2 s/n 3811204, piloted by 1st Lt Bogdan Budzyński, an engine failure occurred. The pilot retracted the landing gear and made an emergency landing on a field near the air base. The aircraft was sent for overhaul to No. 2 Aviation Repair Works in Bydgoszcz. This aircraft had seen intense service for five years, thus it had logged more than 932 flight hours. Despite the fact that the damage sustained during the forced landing was not heavy, it was not overhauled in Bydgoszcz but scrapped. Its components were probably used as spare parts for other aircraft in service.

Until October 1953 only UTB-2 s/n 3811810 remained in the inventory of the 7. PLB. In November 1953 it was transferred to the 3rd Long Range Reconnaissance Squadron of the 21st Reconnaissance Aviation Regiment, where it joined three Tu-2S aircraft, acquired by the regiment previously. After brief service at the regiment's airfields in Sochaczew and Ławica, on 11 August 1954 it was transferred to the Dęblin school, where it received the tactical number "20". The number of UTB-2 aircraft operated by the school increased to nine. From then on the UTB-2 aircraft were operated only in the flying school.

When the first Il-28 jet bombers and their trainer variants UIl-28 entered service in August 1955, the suitability of UTB-2 aircraft as trainers was already limited. Moreover, service life of these intensively operated trainers was expiring. In 1955 four aircraft, 3811806, 3810406, 3810605 and 3811603, were retired.

On 10 August 1956 a dangerous accident with UTB-2 s/n 3811805 took place in a flight maneuvering zone over Wola Klasztorna. 1st Lt Jan Gilos made a turn and then Capt. Michał Sołtowski took over the controls. He executed a full right-

[105]: *Groundcrew working on an ASh-21 engine with removed louvres, adjusting engine cooling.*

hand combat turn and then, when he was commencing the left-hand combat turn at an altitude of 800 m and speed of 300 km, the port engine with half of its mount broke apart. Capt. Sołtowski managed to make an emergency landing on a meadow near Dęblin, near the train station. The aircraft was scrapped. This engine broking apart in flight instigated a decision about withdrawal of worn-out UTB-2 aircraft from service. During their service in the Polish Air Force the UTB-2 aircraft had no fatal crash. In October 1956 the remaining aircraft were retired. Unfortunately, none was preserved for museum purposes.

Colors and markings of Polish UTB-2 aircraft

The UTB-2 aircraft wore a similar paint scheme to the Tu-2S bombers late in their service. Upper surfaces of the wings and fuselage, sides of the fuselage and both tailfins were olive green. Lower surfaces were painted light blue. The checkerboards were of similar size and painted in the same places as on the Tu-2S. Early in their service the aircraft had spinners, which are visible in the photographs. The spinner tips were white or white and red. Later the UTB-2 aircraft were operated without spinners. Initially the UTB-2s operated by the Dęblin school

[106]: *An UTB-2 being refueled from a BZ-43 bowser on a ZiS-5V truck chassis, Dęblin 1954.*

had white single-digit numbers preceded by the letter S painted on the outer surfaces of the vertical stabilizers, for example S-1 or S-7. Later, after the change of the tactical numbers the Dęblin UTB-2s were marked with large, white two-digit numbers. The new numbers were painted on the fuselages aft of the checkerboards on airplanes with numbers 21 and 27, while on airplanes with numbers 23, 24, 25 and 26 they were painted ahead of the checkerboards.

[107]: Cockpit hatch with folding three-step ladder of slightly different design

[108]: A ¾ front view of two UTB-2 aircraft. On the aircraft standing on the right the asymmetry of the nose glazing is visible. It is the only photograph of a Polish UTB-2 on which the asymmetry, albeit not very distinctly, is visible. It is a pity that Zbigniew Chmurzyński did not take a similar photograph from a closer distance.

[109]: Front view of the UTB-2P prototype with visible asymmetry of lower panels of the nose glazing. It was a characteristic feature of all UTB-2 aircraft.

[110]: Sukhoi UTB-2 "S-4" of Officer Flying Training School No. 4, 2nd Training Squadron, 1950. Two-tone paint scheme, olive green and light blue. The aircraft has the first variant of markings with single-digit number preceded by the letter S. Spinners covering the propeller hubs have white and red tips.

[111]: Air-to-air photograph the UTB-2s "S-4" and "S-7" taken from the cockpit of a third aircraft, in flight at an altitude of 400 m near Dęblin in May 1950.

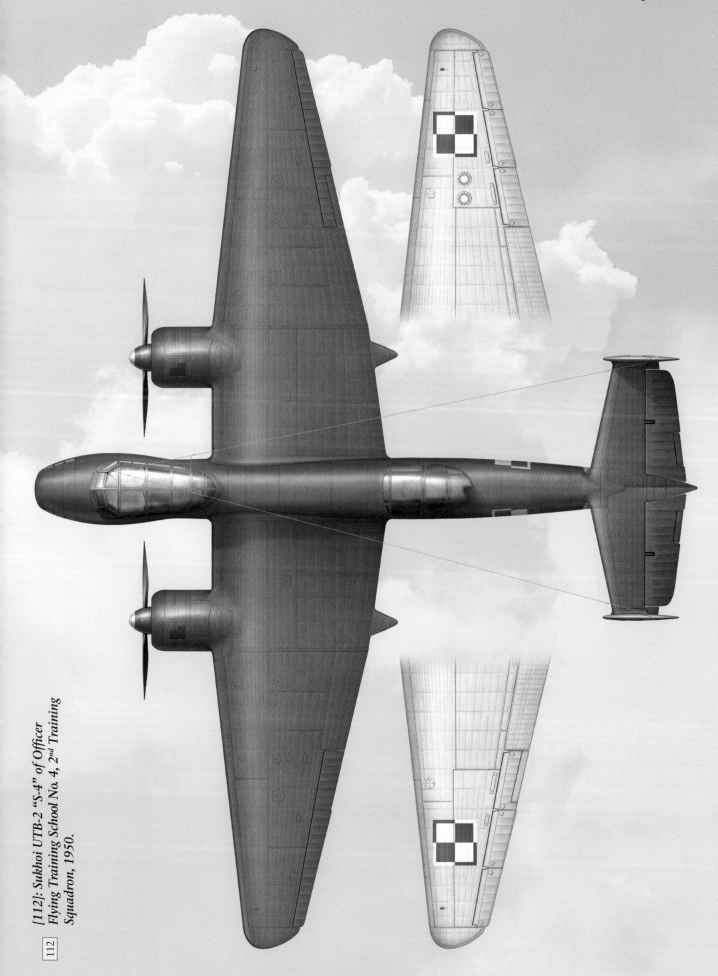

[112]: *Sukhoi UTB-2 "S-4" of Officer Flying Training School No. 4, 2ⁿᵈ Training Squadron, 1950.*

112

Polish Wings

[113]: Sukhoi UTB-2 "24" of the 1st Bomber Pilot Training Squadron, Officer Flying Training School No. 4, Dęblin 1954. Upper and side surfaces are olive green and lower surfaces are light blue. Darker shade of olive green on the fuselage side between the wing trailing edge and checkerboard is probably a result of a repaint. Two-digit tactical number is painted on the fuselage ahead of the checkerboard.

[114]: Air-to-air photograph of UTB-2 aircraft with tactical numbers "24", "21" and "27" (the airplane partially visible in the background). Flights in four-ship formations were among the last exercises in the UTB-2 training syllabus in the Dęblin school.

113

114

[115]: Sukhoi UTB-2 "21" of the 1st Bomber Pilot Training Squadron, Officer Flying Training School No. 4, Dęblin 1954. White tactical number is painted on the fuselage aft of the checkerboard. Upper and side surfaces are olive green and lower surfaces are light blue. This airplane, like the other UTB-2s, flew at that time without spinners.

[116]: A formation of UTB-2 aircraft in flight over the ice-bound Vistula river near Dęblin. The last airplane in formation is "21". The photograph was taken from a fourth aircraft of this type.

115

116

Shcherbakov Shche-2

The need to develop a lightweight transport aircraft, useful in tactical aviation units, emerged in the USSR during the Second World War. As the intensity of the hostilities increased, the need for repairs of damaged aircraft and deliveries of spare parts and ordnance for aircraft increased too. Frontline units needed quick deliveries of new engines and on-time replacements of engines with TBO expiring. Data about the TBO of the engines provides information about the frequency of engine changes. For instance, M-105P engines used in Yakovlev fighters had a time to the first overhaul of 250 hours. However, in heavy frontline conditions these engines needed to be changed after 100 hours. Likewise, the M-82 engines of La-5 fighters also had a TBO of 100 hours. Therefore, urgent deliveries of new engines and spare parts straight to the provisional airfields were necessary. Possible use of U-2 (Po-2) and R-5 biplanes for these purposes was limited. Heavy and large items could not be carried in containers suspended under the wings of these aircraft. For transport of new or overhauled wings the R-5 biplanes were sometimes used, carrying such loads beneath the fuselage. However, engines or antitank guns could not be

carried that way. Obsolete and weary Tupolev G-1 and G-2 aircraft proved useless. In a situation of constant shortage of transport aircraft the few Li-2 aircraft were sometimes used for these purposes and to lesser extent the smaller Yak-6 aircraft, of limited usefulness. Work on the design of a new aircraft suitable for these tasks, initially designated TS-1 (transportnyi samolyet-pervyi, which stands for Transport Aircraft – One) commenced in the autumn of 1941 in the design bureau of Factory No. 482 off Moscow, supervised by Alexei J. Shcherbakov. Taking into consideration the difficulty and complicated conditions of introduction of a new aircraft into production during the war, the designers decided to develop an aircraft built from non-strategic materials and to adopt simple design solutions. It was decided to use proven, already in production and use, aircraft components and devices. In the fixed landing gear shock absorbers from the La-5 fighter were used. The tailwheel was taken from Il-2 attack aircraft. In the design phase the use of two 240 hp German Argus engines was planned. However, the availability of these engines was minimal. The only available, much less powerful, Shvetsov

[117]: The first Shche-2 delivered to the Polish Air Force, assigned to the 13th Independent Transport Aviation Regiment. It wore typical wartime Soviet national insignia – red stars on lower wing surfaces, fuselage and tailfin, as well as large Polish checkerboards on the forward fuselage. The aircraft wears Soviet camouflage, with upper surfaces painted in blue grey and dark grey disruptive pattern. Lower surfaces and fuselage under the wings are light blue. The tactical number "1" was painted on the vertical stabilizer. Ułęż airfield, 1945.

117

[118]: Shche-2 "2" in wartime paint scheme, with four white and red checkerboards in four places. The checkerboard below the cockpit is a remnant of the previous paint scheme. The remaining checkerboards replaced the red stars. Large white number "2" was painted on the fuselage and yellow number "2" from the previous paint scheme was left on the rudder. Warsaw-Mokotów airfield, 2 September 1945.

M-11D 115 hp engines, used in Po-2 and UT-2 aircraft, had to be used. To reduce drag produced by the engines Townend rings were used, in the USSR known as "NAKA" (NACA) cowlings. The fuel was carried in four tanks with a total capacity of 850 l. Two tanks were mounted in the engine nacelles and the other two in detachable outer wing panels. Knowing that the engines would make the aircraft underpowered, it was decided to reduce drag produced by the fuselage to maximise performance. The cross-section dimensions of the fuselage were reduced to achieve a streamlined shape. The cockpit had a similar streamlined shape. The wing bracing struts and struts of the fixed landing gear were covered with fairings. The main wheels were spatted. The aircraft was designed to have an all-wooden braced high wing. To facilitate landing on short strips, the wings were fitted with slotted flaps, lowering to 36 degrees. As it turned out, these flaps significantly lowered the landing speed and shortened the landing roll to 160 m. Semi-monocoque fuselage had plywood skin covered with fabric. Aft of the cockpit was the cargo hold section, with dimensions of 1600 x 1700 mm in its forward section and 6,750 mm long. On the port wall of the cargo hold a large cargo door, 1.43 x 1.64 m, hinging upwards, was situated. Inside the cargo door was another smaller door opening inside and dismantled for parachute dropping sorties. Strengthened floor of the cargo hold was suited for carrying heavy, concentrated loads, such as combat aircraft engines. The aircraft had rectangular wing center sections fixed to the fuselage and detachable, single spar trapezoid outer wing panels, reinforced with two auxiliary spars. The horizontal stabilizer was braced with N-shaped struts fitted to the rear fuselage. Double tailfins were braced against the horizontal stabilizers with single struts. The port rudder was fitted with a trim tab. The TS-1 had seven double folding seats fitted to the fuselage frames and two single seats in the back of the cargo hold. The cargo hold could be used in several variants to carry 14 passengers, 8–10 parachutists or a load of 900–1,150 kg. Ability to carrying standard fuel barrels was also provided. When necessary, in the cargo hold nine wounded could be carried on stretchers mounted on the starboard wall, three in a row on three levels. Each variant of the cargo hold interior could be quickly transformed into another, depending on actual needs. The crew, depending on the mission, comprised the pilot and navigator or flight engineer.

The TS-1 prototype, built in Factory No. 482, was first flown by the factory test pilot V.P. Fedorov in early February 1942. The aircraft had excellent flight characteristics, both in the cruise and landing phases, stability and control response. In late July it was demonstrated to the representatives of the Soviet Air Force in cargo transport, paratrooper/cargo transport and medical transport versions. In August 1942 the TS-1 underwent state evaluation under supervision of test pilot A. K. Dolgov. It was decided that it met frontline requirements for a medium-lift transport aircraft and was cleared for series production. Until then there were no such aircraft in the USSR and the front urgently needed them. After minor modifications and refinements the aircraft entered production in 1943 as the Shche-2. The production was launched in Factory No. 47 in Chkalov (now Orenburg). The chief designer of this factory was Alexei Shcherbakov. Factory No. 47 had terminated production of Yak-6 light twin-engine aircraft, which failed to receive recognition and play a significant role in the Air Force. The prototype of the Yak-6NBB light night bomber also did not arouse interest of the Air Force. A total of 381 Yak-6 liaison aircraft, capable of carrying four passengers or 500 kg of payload, was built. Since these aircraft looked like downsized Douglas DC-3s, license-built as the Li-2, they were called Duglasyonok (Baby Douglas). Thanks to similar technology, switching from production of the Yak-6 to Shche-2 aircraft in Factory No. 47 posed no difficulties. In the spring of 1944 a production Shche-2, s/n 03147, underwent evaluation at NII VVS, which confirmed the previously attained characteristics. In comparison with the prototype TS-1, the production Shche-2 had many improvements. Cargo hold floor was strengthened, balancing of ailerons and landing gear shock absorbing were improved. The shape of the vertical stabilizer was changed and the wingspan was increased. The production rate of Shche-2 quickly increased. In 1944 a total of 222 aircraft were built, and 285 the next year. A further 60 were built in 1946, when production of the Shche-2 ended. A total of 567 Shche-2 aircraft were built in three variants: transport, for carrying passengers or 900–1,150 kg payload, paradropping for 8–10 parachutists, and for navigator/wireless operator training.

After the introduction of the Shche-2 into production the design bureau did not stop refinement work. In October 1944 NII VVS commenced state evaluation of the Shche-2 trainer, s/n 08247, in which the leading engineer A. P. Sharov and test pilot V. S. Kholopov took part. This aircraft was built in Factory No. 482, designed by Shcherbakov in response to ADD (*Aviatsya Dalnego Dyeystva* – Long Range Aviation) demand. It was expected to be suitable for pilot and wireless operator training. In November 1944 another Shche-2, s/n 11547, was sent to NII VVS for further trials. It was converted from a production aircraft built in Factory No. 47. As result of the testing of both these aircraft a more universal variant was put into production. It could be used both for navigator and wireless operator training. It was fitted with RPK-2 or RPK-10 direction finder and RSB-3bis wireless set. It could carry groups of 5–8 trainees with instructor.

The last Shche-2 variant was modified s/n 422047. The number 47 denoted Factory No. 47. The aircraft, built in Factory No. 47 in 1945, was designated Shche-2TM. In modified engine nacelles M-11FM engines, uprated to 145 hp, were installed. The wingspan was reduced by 2.35 m, thus the wing area was reduced from 63.9 to 54.9 m^2. The shape of the vertical stabilizers was changed and the area of the vertical and horizontal empennage was reduced. The flaps were removed and the wing struts were shortened from 3.21 m to 1.965 m. The internal volume of these wing struts served as compressed air bottles. Forward wing fuel tanks were removed, thus the fuel capacity was reduced. The wheel struts were shortened and wheels of smaller diameter were used. Bulged cockpit windows were replaced with flat ones. Cargo hold floor reinforcements between the 9th and 10th frames were removed. These changes necessitated the adjustment of the aircraft's trim. The Shche-2 s/n 422047 was sent to the NII VVS without having conducted static tests,

which in consequence did not allow for conducting the full scope of state evaluation and qualifying it for series production. Tests conducted despite this revealed improvement of the flight characteristics in comparison with production aircraft. This stage of trials was conducted by Eng. A. P. Sharov and test pilot V. S. Kholopov. Tests of aircraft with three types of fixed-pitch propellers and with variable-pitch propellers were also conducted. VISh-327-D210 propellers proved best. However, the Shche-2TM was not put into production, mainly due to gradual limitation of production caused by the end of the war. Due to the same reason, tests of experimental Shche-2 aircraft with GMC Diesel engines (from American combat vehicles), which commenced in July 1945, were not completed.

Production Shche-2 aircraft were unsophisticated in handling. They gained the frontline nickname "Shchuka". In the opinion of test pilot Mark L. Gallai, the Shche-2 had low wing loading, with good flight characteristics, was easy to fly, stable, with quite spacious fuselage. However, it had one main disadvantage, resulting from the fact that the designer had planned that the aircraft be powered with, as it turned out unavailable, 240 hp German Argus engines. The only available, far less powerful, five-cylinder M-11 radial engines rated at only 115 hp were installed instead, so the aircraft flew only at "half power". Therefore it had a long take-off run and attained low altitude. According to M. Gallai the Shche-2 "barely flew on two engines and flying on one engine was totally out of the question". M. Gallai expressed this opinion after a flight he made on this type in the autumn of 1944. He took off from Kaunas with a flight engineer and one important passenger aboard, heading for Moscow. An engine failure occurred near

[119]: *Parachutists before boarding the Shche-2, tail number "2".*

[120]: Shche-2, tail number "3", serial number 061947, in wartime paint scheme and markings. Ułęż airfield, 1945.

[121]: Port side view of the Shche-2 "3" with the upper wing surface visible.

Vyazma. The airplane, flying at an altitude of 50 m, swerved to the right. Fortunately the pilot managed to land on a small forest clearing he had spotted. The starboard engine disintegrated in flight, so that only metal "buckwheat" remained, as Gallai described. Gallai and the passenger made the rest of their journey in a GAZ AA (licence – built Ford AA) 1.5 ton truck to the nearest train station and then by train to Moscow.

Contrasting with this opinion of an experienced test pilot, who first flew prototypes of MiG-9 aircraft, are texts published by Polish authors in 1976 and 1978. They wrote about the Shche-2 that "it could fly even on one engine". According to another publication "without payload this aircraft could fly at low altitude on one engine". Taking into consideration the high power loading (ca. 23 kg/hp) with 115-hp M-11D engines the capabilities of Shche-2 described above were improbable – as it often was in "those days" in descriptions of performance of aircraft originating from the USSR.

Polish airmen had their first contact with the Shche-2 in June 1944. A group of Poles was trained on these aircraft in radio navigation at the 2nd Military Navigator Training School at Chkalov (now Orenburg) on the Ural river. The first Shche-2 was delivered to Poland in February 1945 and assigned to the

13th Independent Transport Aviation Regiment, where it was operational by late May 1945. In March 1945 the Polish Air Force received a further four Shche-2 aircraft. Two were assigned to the 15th Reserve Aviation Regiment *(15. Zapasowy Pułk Lotniczy – 15. ZPL)* based at Radom. The remaining two were assigned to the Military Pilot Training School *(Wojskowa Szkoła Pilotów - WSP)*, established in Dęblin in April 1945 in place of the pre-war Aviation Officer Training Center. The Shche-2 aircraft were ferried to Dęblin by Soviet instructors, assigned to the school. In May 1945 practical training of wireless operators, navigators and aerial gunners commenced in the 4th Training Squadron of the WSP, therefore as early as March 1945 all Shche-2 aircraft were transferred to the Dęblin school. Apart from navigator training, the Shche-2 aircraft were also used for parachute training. During the first post-war celebration of the Aviation Day and air show over Warsaw-Mokotów airfield on 2 September 1945, a mass drop of 39 parachutists from four Shche-2 aircraft was demonstrated. The beautiful view of creamy-white canopies in a blue sky aroused public enthusiasm. There was a great ovation and the spectators, previously calmly watching the airshow, hurried en masse towards the landing parachutists to see them at close quarters.

In April 1946 a Shche-2 from the Dęblin school made a long range (for the capabilities of this aircraft) flight over a 500 km route from Dęblin to Szczecin (previously Stettin in Germany). Three days later it made a return flight to Dęblin. These two flights were described by Col. Czesław Gagajek in his navigator's logbook. He wrote a lot about conditions and circumstances of flying at that time, now arousing wonder or disbelief. Here is the description of these flights:

On 12 April 1946 a delegation from the Military Pilot Training School was sent to Szczecin to participate in the celebration of the first anniversary of the return of the Western Territories to Poland. The name of the Dęblin school was changed the next month (on 17 May) to *Oficerska Szkoła Lotnicza Wojska Polskiego* (Aviation Officer Training School of the Polish Army). Warrant Officer Czesław Gagajek was appointed the head of the delegation and "the navigator responsible for leading the aircraft to Szczecin". The Shche-2 pilot was 1st Lt Kremyen (a Soviet officer) because "he knew the aircraft best and none of the Polish pilots in the school had flown it previously". The chief navigator of the 4th Training Squadron, Capt. Danilchenko (another Soviet officer), emphasized the necessity of good preparation for the flight: *"You must prepare for the flight*

122

[122 – 123]: Shche-2 "4" in wartime paint scheme, but with Polish markings. This airplane had a more extensively glazed cockpit. The nose was painted red.

123

[124]: *Parachutists boarding Shche-2 s/n 51947 before a mass drop during an air show. Warsaw-Mokotów airfield, 2 September 1945.*

[125]: *A fragment of the Shche-2, s/n 18947, probably with yellow nose.*

well. None of you knows this land. We don't even know where the Szczecin airfield is. We haven't got good maps either, only German staff maps". The map received from the squadron chief navigator was a captured top secret huge *Wehrmacht* staff map. It was in 1:1,000,000 scale – 1 cm on the map was 10 km of terrain. It encompassed the entire Central Europe, from Stockholm in the north to Rome in the south, the line Minsk (Belarus) – Bucharest in the east and line Hamburg – Florence in the west. It was of little use for aerial navigation and W/O Gagajek used it only to plot a course from Dęblin via Bydgoszcz and Piła to Szczecin. The Shche-2 took off on

13 April, a few minutes past 10am. The Shchuka (this Russian nickname of the Shcherbakov aircraft was adopted in Poland as well) was loaded with maximum fuel, carried in additional tanks, and eight people on board: the pilot and flight engineer (a Soviet NCO), the navigator, W/O Czesław Gagajek, two flight instructors from the 3rd Training Squadron, W/O Irena Sosnowska and W/O Władysław Rusin, and three officer cadets from training squadrons.

The heavily loaded aircraft slowly taxied on the damp airfield. The pilot taxied to the far end of the airfield to have enough space for a long take-off roll. The Shche-2 rolled

[126]: A Shche-2 pushed on the airfield by trainee parachutists.

on the wet ground at maximum power of its two engines, gaining the speed very slowly, to lift off at the last moment just over the rooftops of Irena (a township adjoining the airfield, renamed Dęblin in 1954). The pilot took a heading for Bydgoszcz, then Piła and then Szczecin. A northwestern wind reduced the aircraft's ground speed to about 100 km/h, which suggested that the flight would take nearly five hours. The aircraft had no radio and the crew had to "fly on time, compass and visual navigation based on the German 1:1,000,000 map". After three hours of flight at an altitude of 800 m the Shche-2 crossed the Noteć river, which once had been the border between Poland and Germany. Devastated villages and towns with ruins, heaps of rubble, ashes and bent remains of constructions, which were the aftermath of the war, moved slowly below. After four hours of flight a great lagoon appeared on the horizon and the contours of the city of Szczecin became visible. The airplane was flying over the wide delta of the Oder river, and flew over the port and made a great circle over the city. The crew were looking for the airfield, but in vain. On the west bank of the Oder, on which the city was spreading, the airfield was not found. The Shchuka turned back towards Dąbie lake. On the German map a small aircraft silhouette was placed near the lake, so the navigator was trying to convince the pilot that the airfield should be nearby. Flying over the lake the aircraft descended to 200 m and the crew were looking for the airfield. On the edge of the water the ruins of a hangar and a building which could be an airport were spotted. An Li-2 and another high wing liaison aircraft stood nearby. Next to the buildings a large crowd, a line of cars and shining instruments of a military band were visible.

The pilot did not know where to land because he saw water, marsh and puddles everywhere. He made a second circle over the marsh, looking for a dry piece of land. People on the ground guessed what problems the crew had and someone ran out of the airport building, waving white flags. Pilot Kremyen understood and commenced an approach for landing. A green flare was fired from the ground. Among the water puddles white letter "T", showing the direction of landing, was visible. Another green flare ensured that there was no threat of overturning. When the airplane's wheels touched the ground, it looked like a floatplane landing. Water was splashing from under the wheels and a long trail of water spray rose behind the airplane. The surface of the airfield proved hard enough so that the Shche-2 ended successfully the landing roll and taxied to the airport without problems. It was 14:55 hours, after nearly five hours of flight. Before departing Dęblin the crew had not received any information about the Dąbie airfield they landed at. It turned out that the airfield was located on the right bank of the river Rogalica, an eastern tributary of the Oder, about 2 km away from Szczecin. The airfield was waterlogged and partially flooded by spring waters of the river and Dąbie lake. The edge of the airfield was hard enough that transport aircraft could land on it. In early April "Polish Airlines LOT had already settled there, opening a permanent route Warsaw – Poznań – Szczecin. There is a radio station and small technical section. We did not have this information when departing Dęblin."

The next two days of the Dęblin school airmen's stay in Szczecin passed in the participation in demonstrations under the banner "We keep guard on the Oder" and a military parade on Grunwaldzki Square. The delegation returned to Dęblin on

16 April. Over the previous three days the airfield had dried and the nearby backwater decreased. Unfortunately, the crew did not manage to refuel the aircraft. "We have no reserves, announced the LOT airport manager, granting clearance for take-off on the crew's own responsibility." The crew assessed that there should be enough fuel to reach Bydgoszcz. The aircraft took off at 10:55 hours to the west to fly once again over the devastated city and destroyed port to bid farewell to Polish Szczecin. After having passed Piła, the aircraft was flying over Krajna, navigator Czesław Gagajek's native region. At his request the pilot descended to 300 m and made two circles over the navigator's family home. The navigator threw a previously prepared sack containing a greeting letter, ballasted with a piece of wall from the ruins of Szczecin, through a sliding window in the cockpit. The sack fell on a field near the house, but was found only a few months later, in summer, during the harvest. At 13:15 hours the Shche-2 landed at Bydgoszcz to refuel. "There were some problems, because in the flight plan the landing in Bydgoszcz was not mentioned. Eventually our landing was considered an emergency and the aircraft was refuelled. We did not expect such formality in the Bydgoszcz-based attack regiment". After one hour and ten minutes at Bydgoszcz airfield, the aircraft took off to Dęblin, covering this route in three hours, ending this trip, unusual and long for the realities of "those times".

The Shche-2 aircraft, which from March 1945 were in the inventory of the 4th Training Squadron of the Aviation Officer Training School at Dęblin, had serial numbers 13947, 15947, 18947, 51947 and 61947. (The number 47 at the end of the serial number stood for the number of Chkalov production facility, which manufactured these aircraft). The aircraft operated in Poland differed between each other in placement, size and number of windows in the cargo hold. In two preserved photographs of the Shche-2 aircraft, additional glazing panels in the cockpit roof are visible. All Polish Shche-2 were operated without NACA cowlings and wheel spats. In the autumn of 1946 three of five Shche-2 aircraft were heavily damaged by a storm. Due to the low flight time left on the damaged aircraft they were deemed non-repairable and were not sent for overhaul. During October 1946 – February 1947 only two remaining aircraft were listed in the inventory of the Aviation Officer Training School. The last Shche-2 was decommissioned in October 1947. Unfortunately none was preserved for museum purposes, only the photographs remained.

Shche-2 aircraft in Poland

Serial number	Known Tactical number
13947	
15947	
18947	
51947	
61947	"3"

[127]: Partial view of four Shche-2 aircraft. The photograph was taken on 2 September 1945 at Mokotów airfield during the air show. Note different sizes of checkerboards on the fuselages and placement of tactical numbers. The disruptive pattern on the wings is similar.

127

[128]: Shche-2 tail number "2" of the Military Pilot Training School at Dęblin in 1945. The aircraft wears wartime paint scheme with upper and side surfaces painted in blue grey (AMT-11) and dark grey (AMT-12). Surfaces visible from below and fuselage under the wings are light blue (AMT-7).

[129]: Shche-2 tail number "2", with three checkerboards on side surfaces and large white number "2" on the fuselage. The checkerboards are painted in place of the red stars. The checkerboard under the cockpit window and yellow number "2" on the rudder are remnants of the previous paint scheme.

128

129

[130]: *Shche-2 tail number "2" with the checkerboard on the nose removed, operated by the Military Pilot Training School at Dęblin in 1945. The aircraft wears wartime paint scheme with upper and side surfaces painted in blue grey (AMT-11) and dark grey (AMT-7). Surfaces visible from below and fuselage under the wings are light blue (AMT-12).*

130

[131]: *Shche-2 "2" with the checkerboard on the forward fuselage and yellow number "2" on the rudder removed.*

131

[132]: Shche-2 tail number "3", serial number 061947 of the Military Pilot Training School in wartime camouflage. Upper and side surfaces are painted in blue grey (AMT-11) and dark grey (AMT-12). Lower wing and fuselage surfaces are light blue (AMT-7). The aircraft had wartime Soviet markings of the Polish air units with the checkerboard as a Polish distinguishing mark. The checkerboard on the port is rotated. The serial number 061947 and nose are yellow. Stylized number "3" has a white outline.

[133]: Shche-2 tail number "3" at Ułęz airfield in 1945. The stylized red digit "3" has a white outline. The checkerboard has reversed colour scheme. The disruptive pattern on the upper surfaces is similar to the paint scheme of these aircraft used in the USSR.

132

133

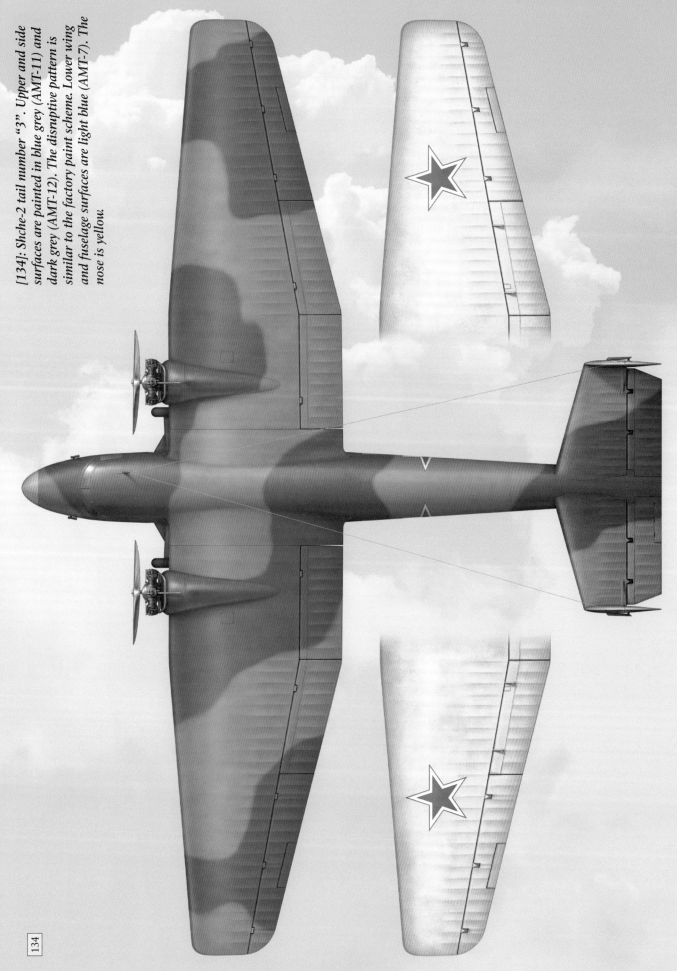

[134]: Shche-2 tail number "3". Upper and side surfaces are painted in blue grey (AMT-11) and dark grey (AMT-12). The disruptive pattern is similar to the factory paint scheme. Lower wing and fuselage surfaces are light blue (AMT-7). The nose is yellow.

134

[135]: *Shche-2 tail number "3" of the Military Pilot Training School in wartime Soviet camouflage and markings.*

135

[136]: *Shche-2 tail number "3", serial number 061947 of the Military Pilot Training School at Dęblin. This aircraft had additional cockpit glazing panels on the top. Ułęż airfield, July 1946.*

136

[137]: Shche-2 tail number "4" of the Military Pilot Training School in wartime paint scheme of two tones of grey (AMT-11 and AMT-12). Lower wing and fuselage surfaces are light blue (AMT-7). The nose is red.

137

[138]: Shche-2 tail number "4" of the Military Pilot Training School in wartime paint scheme of two tones of grey (AMT-11 and AMT-12). Lower wing and fuselage surfaces are light blue (AMT-7).

138

[139]: Shche-2 number "5" in wartime paint scheme. Upper and side surfaces are painted in blue grey (AMT-11) and dark grey (AMT-12). The nose is red. The red stars on the fuselage and lower wing surfaces were painted over, not very carefully, with Polish checkerboards. A small checkerboard of similar size as that on the tailfin is painted on the fuselage.

[140]: Shche-2 "5" of the 15th Reserve Aviation Regiment at Radom airfield in 1945.

141

[141]: *Shche-2 number "5"of the Military Pilot Training School at Dęblin in three - tone wartime paint scheme.*

142

[142]: *The Shche-2 tail number "5"of the Military Pilot Training School at Dęblin. After the aircraft had been transferred from the 15th Reserve Aviation Regiment it had a large checkerboard, the number "5" and yellow nose applied. Dęblin airfield, April 1946.*

Colours and markings of Polish Shche-2 aircraft

The Shche-2 aircraft operated in Poland initially wore a disruptive paint scheme, with upper and side surfaces painted in blue grey and dark grey patches, in accordance with the painting instruction or similar. Surfaces visible from below and the fuselage sides under the wings were light blue. All Polish Shche-2 aircraft initially had typical Soviet markings with large red stars with white outlines on the fuselage, tailfins and lower wing surfaces. Large Polish checkerboards were painted on the forward fuselage, on both sides of the cockpit. The aircraft received individual numbers 1 through 5, painted on the rudders, sometimes using decorative lettering. The numbers were yellow or red with white outline. Noses were painted yellow or red. In 1945 the Soviet markings were replaced with Polish checkerboards. The checkerboards on the forward fuselages were temporarily left in place after the Polish markings had been painted in place of the Soviet stars. White tactical numbers were painted on the fuselages, forward or aft of the checkerboards. Numbers on the rudders were also temporarily left in place. Eventually the checkerboards on the forward fuselage and numbers on the rudders were removed.

[143]: A Shche-2 before a winter sortie, with special covers protecting the cylinders against overcooling.

[144]: Shche-2, s/n 061947 "3". Wire antennae attached to the mast, additional glazing panels on top of the cockpit, outside air thermometer on the windshield and Venturi tube on the side of the nose are visible. Looking through the window is parachute instructor Tadeusz Litwiński.